TO ETERNITY
(and beyond)

Writing Spec Fic Good For Your Soul …

By Michelle L. Levigne

www.YeOldeDragonBooks.com

Ye Olde Dragon Books
P.O. Box 30802
Middleburg Hts., OH 44130

www.YeOldeDragonBooks.com

2OldeDragons@gmail.com

Copyright © 2021 by Michelle L. Levigne
ISBN 13: 978-1-952345-39-5

Published in the United States of America
Publication Date: May 1, 2021

Cover Art Copyright by Ye Olde Dragon Books 2021

All rights reserved. No portion of this book may be reproduced or transmitted in any form or by any electronic or mechanical means, including photocopying, recording or by any information retrieval and storage system without permission of the publisher.

Ebooks, audiobooks, and print books are *not* transferrable, either in whole or in part. As the purchaser or otherwise *lawful* recipient of this book, you have the right to enjoy the novel on your own computer or other device. Further distribution, copying, sharing, gifting or uploading is illegal and violates United States Copyright laws.
Pirating of books is illegal. Criminal Copyright Infringement, *including* infringement without monetary gain, may be investigated by the Federal Bureau of Investigation and is punishable by up to five years in federal prison and a fine of up to $250,000.

Names, characters and incidents depicted in this book are products of the author's imagination, or are used in a fictitious situation. Any resemblances to actual events, locations, organizations, incidents or persons – living or dead – are coincidental and beyond the intent of the author.

TABLE OF CONTENTS

Preface	pg. 1
Introduction	pg. 3
Why Is Science Fiction/Fantasy So Popular?	pg. 11
A Working Definition Of The Genres	pg. 29
Myth, Allegory, And Modern Mythology	pg. 39
"Religious" Vs. "Christian"	pg. 55
Virtues And Vices	pg. 67
The Psychology Of Science Fiction/Fantasy	pg. 85
Christian Fiction And Entertainment	pg. 91
Film	pg. 97
Implications/Conclusions	pg. 105
Sources	pg. 107
About The Author	pg. 111

PREFACE

The original version of this book was actually my Master of Arts thesis in Communications from Regent University, back when it was CBN University. It included a screenplay I wrote to demonstrate my premise, that SF and fantasy could be used as an evangelistic tool, reaching souls where the modern church couldn't reach, speaking a language that many in the church didn't speak. (I won't inflict it on you, but please note that the screenplay will someday be published as a novel set in my Commonwealth Universe SF series, titled **Soloanna.** A good writer never throws out *anything*...)

Essentially, I was arguing against the people who insisted that SF and fantasy and "all that trash" would not only rot my soul, but condemn me to eternal ... well, you know.

If you're reading this book, you've probably had some unpleasant encounters with at least one of these un-enlightened souls who, to be generous, at least *thought* they were well-intentioned. (The amount and quality of that thought is questionable.) Mine occurred in grad school, while I was still formulating my thesis for my Master's portfolio. Inspiration sent by heaven? Hmm, the jury is still out on that. But basically, that attempt to rewrite me to someone else's standards brought me to what you hold in your hot little hands today.

Guess what, gang?

Speculative fiction and fantasy and all the wild and crazy permutations can actually be GOOD for your soul.

I wrote this paper more than thirty years ago, so I know there are many new writings worth referring to that are being left out. I'm not rewriting or adding to this paper. It stands as I wrote it. I thoroughly believe that nothing has changed in terms of the impact that speculative fiction and its many permutations, both delightful and terrifying, can have on your spiritual journey. Yes, it can destroy your soul if you let it. But so can an obsession with fashion, sports, food, music, etc., ad infinitum, ad nauseum.

But consider that because it *can cause harm*, it has the *potential to do great good*. Anything that God created for our enjoyment and benefit, you can bet Satan is going to warp and turn into a weapon against us. And you have to agree with me, the enemy is doing a bang-up job using speculative fiction to further and support his agenda and indoctrinate the masses into following him to their eternal destination.

So maybe ya think we ought to step into the field, and using the same props and set dressing, demonstrate the difference between what he's selling and what we've been sent into the world to share?

Without further ado, I present for your edification:

**TO ETERNITY
(and beyond)**

Previously titled:
CHRISTIANITY AND ALTERNATE UNIVERSES
Presented to the Faculty
CBN University, School of Communication
In Partial Fulfillment of the Requirements of the Master of Arts in Communication
April 1986

Dr. Terry Lindvall
Prof. John Lawing
Prof. Charles Parker

INTRODUCTION

The Problem:

Can Christians write, read, and enjoy the science fiction/fantasy genre without compromising their commitment and walk with Christ? Can this genre be used to the glory of Jesus Christ?

In this paper written in graduate school, I attempted to study the various aspects of science fiction/fantasy, its effects on society, psychology and religious functions, and to answer these questions, if only briefly.

To begin with, it is only logical that wherever Christians are able to work, take enjoyment and come into contact with their fellow human beings, this is a place where seeds can be sown for God's glory.

I felt qualified to carry out a study of the genre, defend it, and explore its potential for Kingdom service because I liked science fiction/fantasy and participated in many activities associated with the genre. This included reading books and stories, watching movies and television programs, club meetings, attending conventions, and at the time of my graduate school studies, writing and producing fan fiction. I am not ashamed to introduce myself as a "recovering Trekker." My first published stories were in fan fiction. I am not as involved in fandom as I once was, but I experienced some of the extremes of fandom, good and bad, encouraging and frightening. While involved in fandom, I noted both the good and bad effects on people, the friendships and rivalries, the giving and the bickering that went on and still goes on behind the scenes. Some may protest that because I was involved, and because I still love the genre, I should disqualify myself from performing such research. But I have to respond: Should someone who *does not* like the genre do the research? Consider the words of C.S. Lewis:

> *Many reviews are useless because, while purporting to condemn the book, they only reveal the reviewer's dislike of the kind to which it belongs. Let bad tragedies be censured by those who love tragedy, and bad detective stories by those who love the detective story. Then we shall learn their real faults. Otherwise we shall find epic*

> *blamed for not being novels, farces for not being high comedies ...*[1]

> *... those who hate the thing they are trying to explain are not perhaps those most likely to explain it. If you have never enjoyed a thing and do not know what it feels like to enjoy it, you will hardly know what sort of people go to it, in what moods, seeking what sort of gratification. And if you do not know what sort of people they are, you will be ill-equipped to find out what conditions have made them so ... you must at least have loved it once if you are even to warn others against it. Even if it is a vice to read science fiction, those who cannot understand the very temptation to that vice will not be likely to tell us anything of value about it ... They will be like the frigid preaching chastity, misers warning us against prodigality, cowards denouncing rashness.*[2]

In this somewhat revised version of my thesis, researched and written in the 80s, I attempt to report both good and evil, the virtues and traps inherent in science fiction/fantasy. It should be kept in mind from the beginning that, as in anything, devotion to a subject depends a great deal on the mentality, personality, and needs of the person involved. Some people enjoy the genre as a light adventure. Others are drawn to the mind-stretching speculation it can inspire. Others devote every particle of their being and energies to it because they have nothing else in life. Should the genre be blamed because people twist and pervert it and let their lives be consumed by it? That's like forbidding all people to write books, because some write pornography. It's like punishing water and bathing because a baby drowned in a bathtub. Science fiction/fantasy, in and of itself, is neither good nor evil: the people who use it, and the uses to which it is put, are what can be labeled good or evil, right or wrong.

C.S. Lewis once wrote, in reference to his Space Trilogy:

---

[1] Walter Hooper. Editor. *C.S. Lewis On Stories and Other Essays*. (Harcourt Brace Jovanovich. NY 1982) pp. 56.
[2] Ibid. pp. 56-57.

... out of about 60 reviewers, only two showed any knowledge that my idea of the fall of the Bent One was anything but an invention of my own. **But if there only was someone with a richer talent and more leisure I think that this great ignorance might be a help to the evangelization of England; any amount of theology can now be smuggled into people's minds under cover of romance without their knowing it.**[3]

Lewis saw a potential for great good in science fiction/fantasy, if used properly. Just as something has a great potential for good, it can also have just as much potential for evil, and thus great care must be taken. As Lewis said elsewhere: "Any road out of Jerusalem must also be a road into Jerusalem."[4]

Some people object to the genre because it speaks of creatures, civilizations, worlds and abilities that do not exist presently, in the known world. In **Perelandra**, the lead character, Ransom, speculates, "Were all the things which appeared as mythology on Earth scattered through other worlds as realities?"[5] Just because something does not exist on known Earth does not mean it *cannot* exist. To extrapolate further, just because something is corrupted and used for evil in one place does not mean it is evil elsewhere; it can be a good, profitable thing if kept to the use it was meant for. Morphine can be used in hospitals to ease suffering, or it can become an addiction and misused until a life is destroyed. God created all things to be good, but His rebellious servants pervert these good things into evil. Perhaps with prayer, searching, and wisdom, all things may be reclaimed for good.

St. Augustine:
[No help is to be despised, even though it come from a profane source.]

But whether the fact is as Varro has related, or is not so, still we ought not to give up music because of the

---

[3] W.H. Lewis. Editor. *Letters of C.S. Lewis.* (Harcourt Brace Jovanovich. NY 1966) pp. 167.
[4] C.S. Lewis. *Christian Reflections.* (Wm. B. Eerdmans Publishing Company. Grand Rapids 1967) pp. 22.
[5] C.S. Lewis. *Perelandra.* (MacMillan Publishing Co. Inc. NY 1944) pp. 145.

superstition of the heathen, if we can derive anything from it that is of use for the understanding of Holy Scriptures; ... For we ought not to refuse to learn letters because they say that Mercury discovered them; nor because they have dedicated temples to Justice and Virtue, and prefer to worship in the form of stones things that ought to have their place in the heart, ought we on that account to forsake justice and virtue. Nay, but let every good and true Christian understand that wherever truth may be found it belongs to his Master;[6]

[Whatever has been rightly said by the heathen we must appropriate to our uses.]

Moreover, if those who are called philosophers, and especially the Platonists, have said aught that is true and in harmony with our faith, we are not only not to shrink from it, but to claim it for our own use from those who have unlawful possession of it. For, as the Egyptians had not only the idols and heavy burdens which the people of Israel hated and fled from, but also vessels and ornaments of gold and silver, and garments, which the same people when going out of Egypt appropriated to themselves, designing them for a better use, not doing this on their own authority but by the command of God, the Egyptians themselves, in their ignorance, providing them with things which they themselves were not making a good use of; in the same way all branches of heathen learning have not only false and superstitious fancies and heavy burdens of unnecessary toil, which every one of us, when going out under the leadership of Christ from the fellowship of the heathen, ought to abhor and avoid; but they contain also liberal instruction which is better adapted to the use of the truth, and some most excellent precepts of morality; and some truths in regard even to the worship of the One God are found among them. Now

---

[6] St. Augustine. *On Christian Doctrine*. **Great Books of the Western World.** Robert Maynard Hutchins, Editor in Chief. (Encyclopedia Brittanica, Inc. Chicago 1952) pp. 646.

these are, so to speak, their gold and silver, which they did not create themselves, but dug out of the mines of God's providence which are everywhere scattered abroad, and are perversely and unlawfully prostituting to the worship of devils. These, therefore, the Christian, when he separates himself in the spirit from the miserable fellowship of these men, ought to take away from them, and to devote to their proper use in preaching the gospel. Their garments, also that is, human institutions such as are adapted to that intercourse with men which is indispensable in this life -- we must take and turn to Christian use.[7]

And to none of all these would heathen superstition ... have ever furnished branches of knowledge it held useful, if it had suspected they were about to turn them to the use of worshipping the One God, and thereby overturning the vain worship of idols. But they gave their gold and their silver and their garments to the people of God ... not knowing how the things they gave would be turned to the service of God.[8]

To extrapolate, Christians are commanded to plunder the "treasures" of the non-believers and take them to be turned back to the proper use of God's service and glorification, which all things were created for in the first place. Countless times, the Israelites were commanded to plunder their conquered enemies and keep what they took. And there were always instructions for what and how much went to the Temple and the priesthood.

Yet, there were also occasions when the Israelites were ordered to destroy all the possessions of the enemy, and not keep even one small coin of the spoil. This can be extended to modern times to apply to Satan's tools of drugs, pornography, profanity, and anything that is not profitable for God's service. These things are perversions, warping away from the true intent of their basic drives.

---

[7] Ibid. pp. 655.
[8] Ibid. pp. 655-656.

Such twisted things only distract from the truth and must be totally wiped out.

Just because some science fiction/fantasy seems to promote occultism or immorality does not mean all the rest is bad. Certain cults use the cross as part of their symbolism, and others use the Bible, with their own twisted interpretations, to foster their false beliefs. Does that mean Christians should stop wearing the cross and reading the Bible? Of course not. It must all be redeemed and use for the good of society and the furtherance of the Gospel. If the good is promoted, the bad will become clear and will be avoided. *At least, this is so in theory*. In actuality, people must be trained to want the good over the evil, to tell the difference between the two opposing forces, and to find the side of light to be more attractive than the side of darkness. If this course is followed for anything in today's society, the false and harmful things can be more readily recognized and abandoned.

George Lucas:
I feel strongly about the role myths and fairy tales play in setting up young people for the way they're supposed to handle themselves in society. It's the kind of thing psychiatrist Bruno Bettelheim talks about, the importance of childhood. I realized ... there was no contemporary fairy tale and that the number of parents who sit down and tell their children fairy tales is dwindling ... unless a child has a very strong family life or is involved with the church, there's no anchor to hold on to ... It's also a psychological tool that children can use to understand the world better and their place in it and how to adjust to that ... Fairy tales, religion, were all designed to teach man the right way to live and give him a moral anchor.[9]

Science fiction/fantasy is stepping in and filling the needs in people's lives that the church and other institutions are not filling, or if they are, not meeting the need adequately. Don't condemn the genre for doing this -- condemn the ones who are not doing their jobs. Christians should study and get involved in science

---

[9] Robert Short. *The Gospel from Outer Space*. (Harper & Row. San Francisco 1983) pp. 49.

fiction/fantasy and all the sub-genres associated with it, so that the uses and abuses can be understood, and either redeemed, turned to their proper uses, or guarded against.

In this book I will *briefly* examine the aspects and implications of the genre and its effect on Humankind and society. I don't expect everyone to agree with the implications and conclusions reached here, or even to agree with the evidence presented. Just think back on all the ridiculous differences of opinion that have split congregations and communities. There will always be those who say something is wrong for Christians because ***they*** don't feel comfortable with it. God works differently with everyone. All His people are individuals. A story will have a desired effect on one group of people, a sermon will have the same effect on a different group of people, and a song will be designed to have the same effect on yet another group of people. God uses many tools. He used Balaam's donkey, so who has the wisdom and authority to dictate His choices in either tools or methods?

Those who come to this book with pre-conceived notions about the genre, movies, literature, Christianity, and how these elements can or cannot work together, and already have their minds made up (meaning they're going to argue if I don't say what they want to hear) will get nothing from this work. Learning only comes to those who are open-minded and ask questions. As I've wanted to say in congregational meetings several times over the years: *Have you considered the possibility that you could be wrong? We're not going to make any progress until you're willing to at least consider it.* (And yes, I need to say this to myself, too!) This book was written simply as an exploration of ideas and possibilities. Those who only look for what they want to find are not being fair either to the subject matter or to themselves. Everyone finds what they look for: good or evil; beauty or ugliness; hope or despair; filth or purity; etc. Those who don't look, won't find.

I am certainly not claiming to be the latest authority on the subject. (Starting with the fact this master's thesis was written going on forty years ago ...) This was and remains only an *attempt* to clarify and discern what has been experienced and learned by my involvement and study of science fiction/fantasy. The boundaries and guidelines to be discussed here cannot and should not be strictly applied to everyone, with no variation. They must be flexible according to the strengths, weaknesses, and needs of the individual.

Because God works differently with everyone. He takes people to the lengths and heights and depths best for them and *no one else*.

Some will not understand what I discuss here, and the conclusions I come to. Some will refuse to understand. Let's close with more wisdom from St. Augustine:

> *To those who do not understand what is here set down, my answer is that I am not to be blamed for their want of understanding. It is just as if they were anxious to see the new or the old moon, or some very obscure star, and I should point it out with my finger: if they had not sight enough to see even my finger, they would surely have no right to fly into a passion with me on that account. As for those who, even though they know and understand my directions, fail to penetrate the meaning of obscure passages in Scripture, they may stand for those who, in the case I have imagined, are just able to see my finger but cannot see the stars at which it is pointed. And so both these classes had better give up blaming me, and pray instead that God would grant them the sight of their eyes. For though I can move my finger to point out an object, it is out of my power to open men's eyes that they may see either the fact that I am pointing, or the object at which I point.*[10]

---

[10] St. Augustine. pp. 621.

WHY IS SCIENCE FICTION/FANTASY SO POPULAR?

A cartoon shows a husband and wife sitting on a couch, watching the television set with a wide-eyed, mesmerized look to them. The wife speaks into the phone without taking her eyes off the set. The caption reads: "We're not here. We've gone out. Try ringing back after 'Star Trek.' This is a recording."[11]

Who would really do such a thing? The truth is, it happens. Fans of Star Trek refer to it as the Sacred Hour (waving hand, Guilty!), sometimes seriously, but most of the time in jest. They don't call each other, answer the phone or doorbell, or allow talking in the room during the airing of the program. Woe betide the rude one who tries to interrupt! (Personal experience here.)

There is concern with the ever-rising popularity of movies, books, TV shows, games, clubs, etc., dealing with the fantastic and "unnatural": Science fiction/fantasy. This concern is mostly over the bad effects of the phenomenon, as well as the amount of time and money spent on both producing and participating in the activities and products related to the genre. And yes, the people who become so lost in their worlds of make-believe that they can't function -- refuse to even try -- in the "real world." (To be fair, everyone wants to run away at one time or another. Right?)

Just why is science fiction/fantasy so popular? And why is this popularity growing?

These questions need discussing for three reasons.

First, a great deal of money, time, and effort goes into the support of the genre each year. Magazines, both professionally and fan-produced, books, technical manuals, art, blueprints, and games are printed and sold in huge volumes. All sorts of products tied into the movie/TV/book universes are produced and sold, such as Star Trek T-shirts, Jedi figures and vehicles, and Alien models; from toothbrushes to jewelry to posters to photographs. The amount of films produced each year in the genre seems to be growing. Re-runs of science fiction TV shows seem more popular than new programs. New fan clubs are started each year, for book series, programs,

---

[11] Patrick Parrinder. "The Black Wave: Science and Social Consciousness in Modern Science Fiction." *Radical Science Journal*. (Vol. 5, 1977) pp. 67.

movies, and individual actors and writers. At the time I wrote this paper, there was an average of twenty conventions each month in the United States alone (and when the world tips closer back to normal, whatever that really is, the numbers will increase -- and don't forget the rising tide of virtual conventions...), and those were just the conventions big enough to have the funds to pay for advertisements in magazines. Fans put in time making costumes and participating in discussions. Most serious of all is the preponderance of role-playing games: not just Dungeons and Dragons, with its very well-publicized disastrous results, but many others based on movies, television, and books, such as James Bond, Dr. Who, Star Trek, World of War Craft, Marvel, Lord of the Rings, etc., ad infinitum. Go into any comic book store and just look at the walls filled with manuals and dice, figurines, cards, etc. Plus, the amount of money spent on computer games, DVDs, and streaming of movies and TV shows.

Second is the concern over the depth of involvement in the genre, sometimes to the exclusion of reality. Of course, there are many more "normal" people involved in fandom than the "unbalanced" and "abnormal." (To be fair, one person's "normal" is another person's "boring," and every fandom thinks all the other fandoms' extreme radical wackos are a lot weirder than their own extreme radical wackos.) The negative aspects do seem to get the lion's share of attention. (And again, to be fair, the negatives in all levels of society, such as religion, business, politics, get more public air time than the reasonable, generous, kind people who make up the majority.) But the *reasons* for the popularity of science fiction/fantasy must be discussed because this genre *does* have such a serious effect. It touches so much of society without people being fully conscious of it. Even in the way they talk: How many people hum the opening bars of Twilight Zone theme music in strange situations or to break tension, or say things like, "It was the logical things to do," or "May the Force be with you," or "Beam me up, Scotty," without really remembering where the phrase started from?

Third: The first step in combatting the negative aspects of the phenomenon, and using the positive aspects to *help* society, is in *understanding* why the genre is so popular, and the effect it has on those who participate in the activities surrounding it.

A good place to start is to study what exactly the genre encompasses, the people who like it, and then figure out the reasons why from the results.

Consider the Preface and Table of Contents of the *Science Fiction Yearbook, Volume One, 1979*, put out by Starlog Press. (Note: I no longer have the book or the photocopy of those pages for reference.) A brief history of the growth of the genre, both in scope and responsibility, was discussed. The Table of Contents showed the wide scope of topics claimed by the genre, things people were interested in. This was not just a gathering of a few fantasy books and special effects movies. Science fiction/fantasy touches art, science, literature, television, and film. The "movement" is big enough to hand out awards for achievement and excellence, hold conventions, and publish a good number of magazines devoted solely to the doings in that one genre. A large following is needed to support such activities. Science fiction/fantasy brings in a lot of money. At the time of writing this paper, I could walk into a handful of brick-and-mortar stores and count at least three science fiction/fantasy-related books among the promoted ten new releases.

I took a random sample from genre-related magazines that were readily available to me at the time I researched my thesis, what I had on hand through subscriptions, and what I could find at libraries, bookstores, magazine stands and specialty stores (comic books, SF stores, gaming supply stores) in the Virginia Beach area. I found seventy-three magazines, from 1971 through 1985, monthly and bi-monthly, with many unavoidable gaps in the series. In all 134 movies/TV shows were discussed in articles, including interviews with actors, directors or other technical people, and discussions of the effects, art, or other work behind the scenes. Some of these were grouped together and counted as one if they happened to be in a series, such as: all the available Star Trek movies and the TV/animated series; the available Star Wars movies and the Ewoks programs; the Indiana Jones films; and the Superman/Supergirl movies. That number of movies and shows make up a good offering of titles, tastes, and story lines for just one genre.

Plus, there were regular columns in the magazines which mentioned these titles and more, commenting on progress in filming or box-office success. *Starlog* magazine had regular columns such as 'Log Entries' for recent doings in all areas of the genre. It and

Fantastic Films had columns for readers to write in and communicate, gripe, praise, or question. There were also areas for reviewing new offerings in the market, such as 'Readout,' (books), 'Soundtrax,' (music), 'Videoscan,' (movies), and 'Videogamz,' (games). *Starlog* offered regular columns where fans could find out what others were doing and try to get in contact with each other. 'Quest' was a column where fans could send in art, comics, poetry, articles, and photos of things they had built or achieved in, related to science fiction/fantasy. And there were semi-regular articles/columns devoted to science-fact, events, and ideas, such as 'Visions.'

A list of general areas discussed shows how diversified the genre is, as well as the interests of the people involved. Related to film, TV, and books, the magazines interviewed/featured: writers, directors, producers, cinematographers, effects people, actors, editors, make-up artists, designers, composers, artists, and illustrators. The history of science and science fiction, literature, and art were discussed. Social problems in futuristic stories, as well as implications of projected new societies and technology were also brought up. This all implies that science fiction/fantasy people aren't the air-headed escapists and mentally/emotionally deficient weirdos they are accused of being, but rather people who think hard and deeply, and who look ahead to the future. As well as the serious side, there is humor and satire, bloopers and comedies that poke fun at sacred cows, such as Star Trek and Star Wars.

The object of the popularity is known. What does it do for people that makes it so popular?

> Science fiction, according to many educators, is interdisciplinary by its very nature, since it covers elements of science, social relations, fantasy, popular art, religion, and many other subject fields. Research and/or curriculum projects utilizing science fiction have been initiated to teach various disciplines including education, science, linguistics, semantics, world history, social studies, and current social issues.[12]

---

[12] John Aquino. *Science Fiction as Literature*. (National Education Association. Washington, D.C. 1976) pp. 15.

Established: Science fiction/fantasy touches many areas of life. The subject matter of the stories takes place in the future, present, and past, touching science, social problems, interpersonal relationships, morals, love, revenge, hate, fear, sickness, etc. In subject matter, it really does not vary much from other genres. The treatment, setting, and hardware are the only truly recognizable variables. But what about the people who like all this?

For one thing, they discriminate. They don't swallow everything handed to them in terms of story, idea, action, etc., just because it is wrapped in science fiction/fantasy. They think. Many types of awards are given to encourage excellence in quality, as well as quantity. They honor their own, as well as being honored by outside forces. They are no longer oddballs who have nowhere to fit in. They are in many fields besides science fiction/ fantasy. In several clubs I belonged to, members included schoolteachers, nurses, night watchmen, Air Force mechanics, bookstore owners, costumers, clerks and college students.

> The audience has certainly become more diverse: among students, for example, SF is as popular with those taking art courses as with scientists and technologists. At the same time, it is increasingly recognized as a force in culture. Some would say that it is becoming 'respectable' (in other words in the academic vogue for science-fiction studies) but it also possess increasing social and political awareness.[13]

The genre is popular because people like the special effects and it satisfies their taste for adventure and spectacle. But it also teaches ideas, gives examples for living, and fills needs.

> When a film such as *The Return of the Jedi* succeeds the way it has, it must do things for people -- provide important gratification, reassurances, fantasies, whatever you will. It is not enough to say that the film 'entertains.' That word tells us nothing. It is what the entertainment does to people -- and for them -- that is of interest.[14]

---

[13] Parrinder. pp. 37.
[14] Arthur Asa Berger. "Return of the Jedi: The Rewards of Myth." *Society*. (Vol. 21, #4. May/June, 1984) pp. 71.

A good deal of fan involvement in science fiction/fantasy consists of writing stories where the fans interact with their favorite characters, play in role-playing and other types of games, or make costumes to dress as a favorite character. Science fiction/fantasy gives heroes to the public in an age of anti-heroes, optimism in a time of pessimism, and someone and something to look up to and identify with.

> ... 'Star Trek' as a program based on moral problems which are stated in the forms of conflict between opposites: the <u>Enterprise</u> crew, reasonably devoted to order and democracy, protecting the weak and innocent, is pitted against the Klingon Empire, which, brutal and self-serving, exploits the weak and innocent. Capt. Kirk, the 'stereotypical ideal of American normalcy,' is the chief mediator when opposing ideals of American society confront one another fictionally. The clarity with which the conflicts of life are presented and resolved in 'Star Trek' may help to explain the cult-like following of viewers that it has generated.[15]

> One of the reasons *The Return of the Jedi* is so popular is that it contains clear-cut series of oppositions that give it meaning. Thus we find the following oppositions in the story: Youth/Old age. Luke/The Emperor. Nature/Technology. Forest/Death Star. The Force/Evil. The Rebels/The Empire. Freedom/Tyranny. Love/Hate. Good Beasts/Bad Beasts. Ewoks/Jabba's Army. The Son/The Father. These oppositions help make the fairy tale understandable to viewers and provide them with easy objects to identify with or despise.[16]

Science fiction/fantasy stretches the mind, with new sights, sounds, actions, and ideas. Many of the writers quoted use terms like "mind-expanding" or "mind-stretching." The genre forces the fans to think in new situations they won't face on Earth. After all, what are the chances of V'ger actually showing up, or a Death Star actually

---

[15] Myles Breen and Farrel Corcoran. "Myth in the Television Discourse." *Communication Monographs*. (Vol. 49, #2. June, 1982) pp. 130.
[16] Berger. pp. 73.

being constructed? (Well, a lot closer than when I first wrote this paper -- but the technology of SF has moved far ahead, too, since then. V'ger is coming closer, but consider that 2001 and 2010 came and the Star Child hasn't showed up yet ...) Bottom line: Science fiction/fantasy shows a new world and more possibilities.

> There's something about science-fiction -- it stretches the mind. After you've spent a few afternoons with Heinlein, Asimov, Sturgeon and Clarke, everything else is mundane. Dull. After you've spent an evening saving the Earth, exploring the galaxy, discovering immortality, probing the depths of the mind, touring the far future and achieving The Answer to it All, who cares about the dishes or the six o'clock news? Once your mind has been thoroughly boggled, you want to keep that sense of wonder -- you don't want to lose the wider horizons that science-fiction has given you.[17]

In the new world created, the viewer/reader/gamer can step to one side and study the world as it is, perhaps seeing new solutions and new problems because he sees through alien eyes.[18]

> Obviously, a lot of modern space fantasy is merely entertainment ... a lot of it is much more than this. Science fiction's best representatives do indeed contain 'mind-expanding, heavy philosophy;' they can help us examine our mundane earthbound problems from a fresh, original viewpoint.[19]

> ... science fiction has immense value as a mind-stretching force for the creation of the habit of anticipation ... they (writers) can lead young minds through an imaginative exploration of the jungle of political, social,

---

[17] David Gerrold. *The World of Star Trek*. (BlueJay Books, Inc. NY 1984) pp. 92.
[18] Ibid. pp. 34.
    Hooper. pp. 48.
    Michael Phillips. Editor. *Philosophy and Science Fiction*. (Prometheus Books. Buffalo 1984) pp. 3.
[19] Short. pp. 15.

psychological and ethical issues that will confront these children as adults.[20]

Science fiction/fantasy can teach through example. IE, Star Trek was a revolutionary idea in the late 60s because it had a multi-national, multi-race, co-ed crew, working together in harmony. A white male was in command, but a black female was fourth in line of command. (And Gene Roddenberry received trouble and complaints from network people and prejudiced viewers because of that.) Star Trek also taught optimism at a time when it seemed the world would not last to the end of the century and showed viewers a galaxy-spanning free Federation working together for the good of all people: Optimism and hope for the future.

Science fiction/fantasy teaches by example when good conquers evil, as in the Star Wars stories. With heroes who have values, who care and make sacrifices for others, viewers learn a real man, or a person of power, doesn't have to be self-centered or cold to succeed.

The genre also brings myth back into its intended function of working out social problems vicariously, of passing on ideas and role models, and bringing back values people can believe in and hope for. Myth explains without being didactic.[21]

> ... to create exemplary models for a whole society in a process that translates a single life-history into an archetype, thereby setting up patterns for imitation ... the screen media plays a similar role in setting up heroes and heroines to carry on mythological tradition.[22]

Science fiction/fantasy reinforces values when the actions of the hero run parallel with current value systems and belief structures.[23]

> The hope, the anticipation of fantasy and mythic literature is that by bringing a power larger than man but apparent through man to bear upon this world, we can once again

---

[20] Aquino. pp. 16.
[21] Wm. Blake Tyrell. "Star Trek's Myth of Science." *Journal of American Culture*. (Vol. 2, #2. 1979) pp. 288.
[22] Breen. pp. 129
[23] Berger. pp. 73.

kindle the light of the human spirit. The nature of that
power ... is constituted of enduring and indomitable
values such as heroism, chivalry, a sense of good over
against evil.[24]

    And when the story runs counter to current values and beliefs, it encourages questioning both the new beliefs, actions, and reasons, and the previously held ones. This questioning will help the person learn and grow -- whether positively or negatively depends on the individual. Some writers use science fiction as social criticism to bring about change *by* causing the fans to question the way things are. Others see science fiction/fantasy as a way of preparing for future change.[25] Think back to the quote from George Lucas about the importance of childhood and fairy tales.[26]
    The genre fills needs: for security, hope, answers, meaning, even religion, that people are not getting elsewhere. Writers attempt to answer questions and problems that they have and have faced, and offer solutions, patterns and examples to those around them, using the characters and situations in their stories to diagram how this answer will ultimately work out.

The fantasies that are undoubtedly being written today ...
will arise from as yet unguessable troublings within
American life. And they will convert those irritations --
not simply cover them over with coats of pearl, but
completely reshape them -- into meaningful narratives
new in insight and richly traditional in form and matter.[27]

If science fiction is an extrapolation from the known into
the unknown, then the *Odyssey* of Homer is science
fiction. Until somebody came back from the western
Mediterranean with an accurate map, no one knew for
certain that the Strait of Mesina wasn't guarded on one
side by a whirlpool and on the other side by a many-

---

[24] John H. Timmerman. *Other Worlds: The Fantasy Genre.* (Bowling Green University Popular Press. Bowling Green, Ohio 1983) pp. 28.
[25] Parrinder. pp. 39.
[26] Short. pp. 49.
[27] Brian Atteberry. *The Fantasy Tradition in American Literature.* (Indiana University Press. Bloomington 1980) pp. 186.

headed monster. As known geography rolled back the unknown frontiers, science fiction (as thus defined) moved with them.[28]

Science fiction/fantasy tries to give security in a world of chaos.[29] It tries to conquer fears by showing archetypal heroes conquering symbols of those fears, i.e., in Star Trek, many episodes showed Kirk battling computers that had taken over societies, turning the people into mindless or heartless creatures. This is a working out of Humanity's fear of machines taking away jobs and the meaning of life. Kirk always won, even when the computers/machines were definitely superior.[30] Many current movies give hope for help, right now, from the skies. Humankind no longer has to wait until they can go to outer space -- outer space comes to him and becomes his friend, ala *ET* and *Close Encounters*.[31]

The mythic element of the genre tries to put meaning back into life, as well as hope for help. If people think they can't surmount their difficulties, they have no hope and no reason to exist. Star Trek recreated the heroic archetype to bring hope and meaning back into life.[32]

> ... psychologists found ... the sense of loss of meaning could result in a host of psychological and physical illnesses. Although not all psychological illness has this root, the loss of direction and purpose is often a common cause of such illness in the modern world.[33]

As well as the psychological help of meaning, the benefits of fantasy help people work out problems, worries, and fears vicariously. Harmful intents are released without hurting anyone. The unconscious is exercised instead of being repressed, and evil is

---

[28] Paul A. Carter. *The Creation of Tomorrow*. (Columbia University Press. NY 1977) pp. 31
[29] Timmerman. pp. 21.
[30] Tyrell. pp. 288.
[31] Short. pp. 32.
[32] Tyrell. pp. 290.
[33] Morton T. Kelsey. *Myth, History, and Faith*. (Paulist Press. NY 1974) pp. 21.

exorcised instead of being allowed to grow until it can no longer be held back.[34]

Science fiction/fantasy fills a need, a hunger, an emptiness in the public. Sometimes the people are aware of it, but most of the time *not*, because they aren't aware of their lack. All they know is that the fantastic fills a need, makes them feel good, and satisfies them. **Could this need be God, and the movies, books, etc., satisfy because they hint at some power or existence beyond Humanity, tasting faintly of God?** Much science fiction/fantasy, upon investigation, has religious elements, flavor, and feel to it. People turn from formal religion because it has hurt them, or their religious leaders do not know how to present it to the people. Turning away from the God of formal religion, people still seek Him in the fantastic. They need Him for a **why**, a purpose in life. If there is no God, then no life after death, and then no real reason for living at all.[35] People don't want God on the terms His people present, but they still need Him, and so recreate Him to fill their specific needs.

> 'Close Encounters' breaks out of the traditional formulae of sci-fi movies, and does so with the help of a mythic understanding of America's need for a secular religion ... for the movie believes there can be a higher authority, a great power which is simultaneously beyond mere material concerns and benevolent toward all.[36]

> People can croak "Entertainment! Entertainment!" until they're blue in the face. The fact remains that films like *Close Encounters, Superman,* and even *Star Wars* have become jerrybuilt substitutes for the great myths and rituals of belief, hope, and redemption that cultures used to shape before mass secular society took over.[37]

Rev. William Boyle:

---

[34] John Aquino. *Fantasy in Literature.* (National Education Association. Washington, D.C. 1977) pp. 10.
[35] Short. pp. 4.
[36] Charles Molesworth. "Some Paragraphs on Close Encounters." *Journal of American Culture.* (Vol. 2, #2. 1979) pp. 263-264.
[37] Short pp. 15.

"I think there's a real longing in people's hearts for the spiritual. There's a natural longing in our hearts for God and our creator, so when you touch on areas of spirituality, I think you see a longing for a meaning outside of ourselves." If that's true, why aren't people lining up outside churches instead of movie theaters? Maybe ... organized religion hasn't been able to communicate that message to the public. Not as well as *ET,* anyway.[38]

Maybe the Church isn't doing its job. God isn't just a list of do's and don't's. God is beauty and abundant life. The Bible paints beautiful word pictures that speak to the soul, not just the intellect of Man. Most of the time, the Church doesn't do what it should, and people aren't fed as richly as they should be. A diet of bread and water is fine, but what about fruit, honey, and wine?

Modern people have no vital mythology, as did the Greeks. The supremacy of the Judeo-Christian philosophy in western people's lives is not what it once was. The authority of SF as myth exists in its roots in modern science. In the absence of myth or religion, people have found solace in fictional science that paints unknown futures where exist the imagined achievement of their waking dreams. And science-fiction does fulfill a function one associates with myth: it fills the reader with a sense of wonder and awe. Its confines are the past, the present, and the future, its base is science, its premise is 'what if?' and its path, the path of imagination.[39]

Why has the hunger shown up so strongly now? These films deal with powers beyond Humanity, worlds they can't form or control. Humanism no longer works. Humankind is not the ultimate power and answer, as had been preached for so long. Dietrich Bonhoffer says: "Man is again thrown back on himself. He has managed to deal with everything, only not against Man. In the last resort, it all turns on Man."[40] And Humankind no longer has all the

---

[38] Ibid. pp. 68.
[39] Aquino. *Science Fiction as Literature.* pp. 21.
[40] Short. pp. 31.

answers. "The present interest in myth reflects a need and search for order and certainty in the midst of the apparent chaos and disorder of the 20th century."[41]

In all this chaos and turmoil of the present age, people feel very helpless and small. They feel useless, unable to control their own destiny. "We will need ... something far greater than ourselves to convince us of our significance. When we say 'I' -- or 'Humankind!' -- in a very loud voice we still haven't said 'God.'"[42] Humanism has failed. Leaving out God has left out purpose from life. Humans are miserable creatures, and if there is not something or Someone out there, the world is in a lot of trouble.

> ... nothing is more demeaning to the human spirit than meaninglessness. Nothing is harder for us to stand than the lack of ultimate understanding ... To an enormous extent, 'Christendom' has turned away from Christ, and no doubt it is for this very reason that there is such a lack of understanding and meaning today in the so-called Christian world ... Strange to say, however, it was largely Christendom's own understanding of Christ that produced this wholesale defection from Christ in the first place. And this happened in two ways:
>
> First, because we began to *mis*understand Christianity as a faith based primarily on *fear*, we became readier to get rid of this harsh, vindictive God and to replace Him ... with some other god ... Secondly, it was largely Christianity itself that paved the way for all of this Western knowledge and means and know-how and reliance on what can be seen. For many Christian correctly understood that if God <u>alone</u> was supernatural, then nature couldn't contain anything supernatural to harm us ... Nature was God's <u>good</u> creation, and therefore nothing to be afraid of. Because of this belief, we were not free to investigate nature and to use its desacrilized reality for our own purposes.
>
> And in this way Christianity undermined superstition and laid the philosophical foundations necessary for the

---

[41] Timmerman. pp. 21.
[42] Short. pp. 7.

rise of modern science and technology. And how modern science and technology rose. And along with them, something else rose -- namely, our confidence in ourselves. And as soon as we obtained this confidence, we felt we had all we needed to chuck the gloomy old God of fear and damnation and make a fresh start. We would throw Him down and elevate our own capabilities to the level of godhood.[43]

So, the Church is just as responsible as the non-believing philosophers for the spiritual trouble the world is in. The Church rarely presents the answer people need, in ways that attract them. A bowl of brown goo may have all the protein and vitamins needed to sustain life and give energy, but if it isn't appetizing or attractive, who will *willingly* eat it? The beautiful and satisfying will be consumed, not what just promises to fill needs, and yet at the same time does not commend itself to the senses. God, after all, made His people with senses and the desire for beauty.

A major draw of the genre is the sense of wonder and beauty it gives, and not just because of special effects. There is some sort of omnipotence, omniscience and other feelings brought through the movies, something beyond human experience and a reason for hope, that was lacking in people's church experiences and relationships with other Christians. Something that should have been there.

It should be emphasized ... lest any misunderstand that the fantasies are not merely anecdotes and illustrations of theological ideas; at their best they are imaginative and symbolic explorations of a vision of the significance of life ... Emotions are not simply described to us; they are created within us. We are made to feel awe in the depths of our beings. The effects that one experiences are those that great myths have always created within man ... to suggest that the open- minded reader may well have moments when he feels himself more near the ultimately Real than he has yet been.[44]

---

[43] Ibid. pp. 2-3.
[44] Rollan Hein. *The Harmony Within.* (Christian University Press. Grand Rapids 1982) pp. xviii.

If these movies give a taste of the needs we have and partially/temporarily fill them (the need is for God, and only God can fill it completely) then people are taking the messages in willingly, which makes it easier to affect people than other things in society can. People want to believe in Mr. Spock and Luke Skywalker. Some are so hungry for the hope and order and a thousand other qualities these heroes represent that these fictional people are often emulated. Wouldn't it make sense to plant seeds of moral strength and beliefs in these works? The results would show up later in a stronger nation. Look how the relaxing of moral codes in the movies, TV, and books have paralleled/resulted in decay in the nation's morality, values, strengths, and patriotism.

People are looking for a key, a reason for living, something to model their lives on. If the key is a book or movie with loose or high morals, that's what they'll follow. Look at *Close Encounters,* where people refused to let anything stand in the way of realizing the answer to their quest. The whole world is like that, to varying degrees, yet only a few realize it. "People's built-in quest for meaning and their looking for the lost key for which they were made, is central to the story of Close Encounters."[45] Humanity is made with a need for God, a need only God can fill before people are fulfilled.[46]

In a sense, because of the answers presented in them, much science fiction/fantasy can be termed religious. "Religion starts with the attempts of our imaginations to cope with reality -- a reality in which the clock is quickly running out for all of us and life tends to be just one rude awakening after another."[47] But the stories fall short of the goal, no matter how beautiful or fulfilling these visions of men's minds are. The need is for God, not some watered-down dream created by someone who probably doesn't know much of the truth. Unless the filmmaker/writer is in touch with God and God's truth, his story will never really satisfy the audience. It can be a story that is wholesome, a fun adventure, and that may be all that is intended, but it will never be as totally satisfying as a story which has the same effects, but with God integral to it. That is because it is from fallible Man, not infallible God.

---

[45] Short. pp. 34-36.
[46] Ibid. pp. 12.
[47] Ibid. pp. 9.

> German theologian, Freidrich Gogrten:
> Of all man's presumptions, that which is commonly known as religion is the most monstrous. For it is the presumption of seeking to bridge over from opposite to opposite, from creator to creature, and to do so by starting from the creature.[48]

    Science fiction/fantasy movies are so popular because they hint at the real answer, reason, and purpose in life that everyone is looking for. Humanism, which preaches man as the answer, has failed. People now look for fulfillment beyond the known world. The future, outer space, aliens, advanced technology and telepathic powers of all kinds hint at the omnipotent, omniscient, omnipresent God. It's like eating junk food that tastes of the real food people need, but with additives and fillers mixed in that aren't needed, and could really be harmful. But that is often the only type of food people know, so they eat and love it, and don't know where the real food is. Possibly they turn away from the real because it is not attractive to them. Christians must invade the world of science fiction/fantasy and take it over, changing it from the inside. Bit by bit, more real "food" must be made attractive and added to the junk, so that people can be weaned away from their junk food diet, and their hunger can really be satisfied, once and for all.

    The stories in the genre illustrate the struggles people go through today, no matter how far off in time and space the setting may be. And because these stories can be related to real experience, they touch the human soul, expressing more intimately beliefs, ideals, hopes and dreams.

> The essence of all religions, from the most primitive to the most highly developed, has always been expressed by the human soul in stories ... We can say, "I believe in this or that," and assert the truth of many doctrines, but these things will not affect the soul of any one of us unless in some way we experience their meaning through intense response to the images conveyed in story. Innumerable tales in all ages have expressed the changing relationships

---

[48] Ibid. pp. 8-9.

of human beings to their gods and have told of their search for the divine meaning behind their lives.[49]

    Science fiction/fantasy covers a wide variety of areas of life, socially, monetarily, in the media, and psychologically. The people who enjoy the genre have no special trait to set them apart from people who don't, except perhaps for a more active imagination or the daring to reach out to impossibilities and make them into possibilities.

    The genre teaches morals and optimism, fights prejudice, criticizes society, and provides examples for people to emulate and follow. (And *rewrites* society, imposes the morals and values of the writers, which can be a negative as well as a positive effect. *Don't condemn the tool: condemn those who use it, and the use to which they put the tool.*) It invents heroes, filling a function of myth when other parts of society do not provide the support and education they are supposed to. Science fiction/fantasy expands the mind by presenting new thoughts in unusual settings and urging people to question the established norm. (Both a positive and a negative. Use carefully!) It also fills needs for hope, security, and meaning in life. When organized religion no longer fills its function, the genre steps in.

    Science fiction/fantasy is also fun.

    Until something can fill needs more thoroughly or the people who support it are disillusioned, they will not be persuaded away from science fiction/fantasy.

---

[49] Helen M. Luke. *The Inner Story*. (Crossroad Publishing Company. NY 1982) pp. 1.

A WORKING DEFINITION OF THE GENRES

If science fiction is an extrapolation from the known into the unknown, then the Odyssey of Homer is science fiction. Until somebody came back from the western Mediterranean with an accurate map, no one knew for certain that the Strait of Messina wasn't guarded on one side by a whirlpool and on the other side by a many-headed monster. As known geography rolled back the unknown frontiers, science fiction (as thus defined) moved with them.[50]

Before the values, failures and uses of science fiction/fantasy can be discussed, a definition of the genre must be formulated. Science fiction is one genre, and fantasy another, but oftentimes the two are combined, as in Star Wars, the Dragonrider stories of Anne McCaffrey, the Apprentice Adept series by Piers Anthony, and C.S. Lewis' Space Trilogy. Just where does science fiction end and fantasy begin? Sometimes, they blend together and never really withdraw to the point where one or the other can be defined. A very rough or broad description would be that science fiction deals with the future, alien planets, advanced or strange technology and different civilizations, while fantasy deals with the past and magic. Long ago, this would have held true, but no longer. See what three experts say about it:

Kingsley Amis:
SF is the class of prose narrative treating of a situation that could not arise in the world we know, but which is hypothesized on the basis of some innovation in science or technology, or psuedoscience or pseudotechnology, whether human or extra-terrestrial in origin.

Sam Moskowitz:
SF is a branch of fantasy identifiable by the fact that it eases the willing suspension of disbelief of its reader by

---

[50] Carter. pp. 31.

utilizing atmosphere of scientific credibility for the imaginative speculations in physical science, space, time, social science and philosophy.

Donald H. Wollheim:
SF is that branch of fantasy which, while not true of present day knowledge, is rendered plausible by the reader's recognition of the scientific possibilities of it being possible at some future date or at some uncertain period of the past.[51]

Even the experts can't totally agree, because it has blended together so well. Since fantasy has been around longer, it is said science fiction is a branch of fantasy, or just a new kind.

Some say science fiction shows where Humanity will be in fifty, 100, or even 1,000 years from now. Some of the predictions are utopian. Some are all bad, standing as warnings to stop what is going wrong now. Science fiction speaks of the possibilities, extrapolated from what is present in this age, from attitudes, ideas, and problems. Much of science fiction can be like any other genre, set apart only by the "toys" and locations, which cannot be found on Earth. Some people ask: Why have the genre at all, if in the long run it is just like the others? For one thing, it is fun. There is nothing wrong with fun, is there? People need escape and relaxation. The settings are fresh, and problems are approached from a new angle. Also, contemporary problems seen in a new setting can perhaps be seen more clearly and worked on with a new attitude.

Ursula K. LeGuin:
Science fiction is not predictive; it is descriptive. All fiction is metaphor. SF is metaphor. What sets it apart from older forms of fiction seems to be its use of new metaphors, drawn from certain great dominants of our contemporary life -- science, all the sciences, and technology and the relativistic and the historical outlook, among them. Space travel is one of these metaphors; so is

---

[51] John Aquino. *Fantasy in Literature.* pp. 10.

an alternative society, an alternative biology; the future is another. The future, in fiction, is a metaphor.[52]

Fantasy is a kind of mythology, a search for an answer in life. Science fiction fills hunger in people that organized religion can't reach. Perhaps it is not recognized as a new religion because the terminology is different.

The world view implied by UFO stories is not religious or mythological, but scientific. We have replaced our divinities with extraterrestrials, who may appear in lore as destroyers or saviors. Our Other World is the rest of the universe and its magic is an advanced form of science. Similarly, in recent American literature, technology takes over the functions of magic, and fantasy transforms into science fiction, a genre with entirely different conventions and aims. SF is predominantly speculative, looking forward and outward. Fantasy is more introspective and traditional; it attempts to revivify old metaphors and reembody old mythologies.[53]

What is it that distinguishes a liking for today's science fiction writers from an enjoyment of J.R.R. Tolkein or of *Watership Down*? Roughly speaking, we may say that both science fiction and fantasy involved the transcendence in the imagination of the existing social and 'natural' order. But this is only valuable where the transcendence involved consciousness of the effort and struggle necessary to achieve it. SF possesses this awareness of struggle through its dependence on the intellectual and cognitive outlook of modern man. The writer has to justify each step that he takes in the creation of his fictional 'parallel world.' In political terms, this concern with the process of construction of a parallel world can be used to invite the reader to conceive of what would be involved in struggling for a better world for himself. Fantasy, on the other hand, offers the results of

---

[52] Dick Allen. Editor. *Science Fiction. The Future.* (Harcourt Brace Jovanovich. NY 1983) pp. 2.
[53] Atteberry. pp. 26-27.

> transcending the existing order without any of the struggle to attain it. In pure fantasy, time is abolished, the causation of events is magical or absurd and consequently everything is possible.[54]

Science fiction sets the common in new settings, so they are sometimes totally unrecognizable, and in studying them people can learn more about the world and themselves. This in itself makes the genre a valuable art form, even without the escape and relaxation that it offers. "As a number of meaning analysts have acknowledged, SF can be a valuable resource in discussions of meanings. SF sometimes describes beings and cultures that are so exotic or alien to us that it is not clear that our ordinary concepts apply."[55] "Some very interesting SF has been written from the standpoint of social trends. Where this is done well, such stories provide us with a detailed picture of what life in a society designed to satisfy the relevant idea would be like. In this way they sometimes help us to understand and to evaluate it."[56]

> Science fiction, according to many educators, is interdisciplinary by its very nature, since it covers elements of science, social relations, fantasy, popular art, religion, and many other subject fields. Research and/or curriculum projects utilizing SF have been initiated to teach various disciplines including education, science, linguistics, semantics, world history, social studies, and current social issues.[57]

Because of the sad shape of the world today, people don't look forward to the future. Either they believe there is no future, or else it will be worse than what is presently available to them. Science fiction takes place mostly in the future or alternate universes, and it gives hope. It says, "We've made it this far, we've solved our problems, life is easier and more comfortable, and now we have the whole universe to explore." Science fiction gives the

---

[54] Parrinder. pp. 43.
[55] Phillips. Editor. pp. 1.
[56] Ibid. pp. 3.
[57] Aquino. pp. 15.

hope that religion should be providing. " ... science fiction has immense value as a mind-stretching force for the creation of the habit of anticipation ... (writers) can lead young minds through an imaginative exploration of the jungle of political, social, psychological, and ethical issues that will confront these children as adults." (Alvin Toffler)[58] It prepares people for the future. But it does not prepare them spiritually, except for things like the Force, or Vulcan disciplines.

Not all science fiction is futuristic. A good portion of the stories take place in the present, either on the known Earth or an alternate universe, to examine what is going on in the world and propose solutions.

> ... SF writers have sought to express current tensions in mythic ways, on the premise that creative imagination is frequently able to give a more comprehensive view of a debate than rational argument can. Despite the SF dictum that stories ought to be postulated on scientific concepts extrapolated from existing data, many stories enthusiastically adapt current technology for their mythical purposes. Nuclear power, for instance, has become 'a metaphor for the nearly magical fashion in which heroic scientists could overcome the inconvenient laws of nature and get space-borne cowboys out to the endless frontiers of inter-galactic space.' With the increasing popularity of the genre through its adoption by film and TV, SF undoubtedly qualifies as a most interesting example of deliberate intervention in the usually hidden cultural mechanisms which generate myths.[59]

Science fiction is not a genre which can be slapped together with a lot of wild imaginings, adventure, and colorful words. At the start of the genre, there was no existing example of science fiction stories available, no "form" to follow. In some ways, there still isn't one, and writers in the genre have to build a frame from the ground

---

[58] Ibid. pp. 16.
[59] Breen and Corcoran. pp. 135.

up, making sure everything supports what comes after it. For any fiction to work, it has to be believable.

SF is not a western with ray guns and spaceships. It is a genre so demanding that few of its practitioners are more than moderately competent at it. The responsibility to be logical and scientifically accurate, while at the same time telling a good dramatic story, will continually defeat any writer who approaches the field with less than total respect for the requirements.[60]

'Hard' science fiction is concerned with extrapolation from current discoveries in the physical and biological sciences. The emphasis is on the engineering applications of these sciences ... 'Soft' SF is more difficult to define than 'hard,' because it is usually seen as a reaction away from {it} ... Evidently there are various stages through which such a reaction can pass. The first involves a movement from the physical to the social sciences and from engineering to more speculative extensions of theory. Then there is an increasing concern with human relationships -- the major preoccupation of literature as a whole. Lastly, all connections with the reasoning and methods of science may be severed, so that scientific ideas become the marginal -- and magical -- accompaniments of an exercise in pure fantasy ... Sociology, anthropology, psychoanalysis and ideologies such as Marxism are as much in the domain of science fiction as are lasers and the laws of thermodynamics.[61]

When all is said and done, science fiction is an off-shoot of fantasy, grown to meet the needs of the times, just as fantasy grew to meet the needs that myth and ritual and other predecessors could not meet.

Science fiction is the contemporary fairy tale, it's the 20th century morality play. At its worst, it's merely romantic

---

[60] Gerrold. pp. 26.
[61] Parrinder. pp. 38.

escapism, but at its very best, it is the postulation of an alternative reality with which to contemplate this one.[62]

Fantasy has been looked down on perhaps even more than science fiction because so much of fantasy deals with magic. Part of the problem is that people insist the fantasy world must be run by the same rules as the real world. It can't be fantasy if it is exactly like the real world (which the people try to escape through books or film). The fantasy world is a metaphor. In a Christian's hands, it is a literalizing of the very real battle between good and evil. It is a spiritual battle of powers. Christians are armored by God's grace. In a very real sense, it *is* magic.

> It may perhaps clarify the issue if we recall that what is now regarded as the 'real' world -- that is, the world of empirical experience -- was for many centuries regarded as the world of 'appearances.' To our ancestors, more inclined than we by belief and by learning to look beyond the material world for reality, the ultimately real lay in spiritual otherworlds. It is with the reality of such otherworlds that fantasy very largely deals.[63]

If one looks closely, a vast majority of stories are not concerned with magic or the magic land, but with the people involved in them, their relationships, concerns, interactions, and the battle of good and evil. The story isn't about magic, per se, but only uses the magic beasts and devices to move the story along. Sometimes the stories are about "normal" people from an "ordinary" world, cast into abnormal circumstances in a world they know nothing about. The fairy of fairy tales is just as much a setting as the *Enterprise* or Dodge City.

> Most good fairy-stories are about the adventures of men in the Perilous Realm or upon its shadowy marches. Naturally so; for if elves are true, and really exist independently of our tales about them, then this is also certainly true: elves are not primarily concerned with us, nor we with them. Our fates are sundered, and our paths

---

[62] Gerrold. pp. 34.
[63] Ann Swinfen. *In Defense of Fantasy*. (Routledge & Kegan Paul. Boston 1984) pp. 11.

seldom meet. Even upon the borders of Faerie we
encounter them only at some chance crossing of the ways
... a 'fairy-story' is one which touches on or uses Faerie,
whatever its own main purpose may be: satire, adventure,
morality, fantasy.[64]

A fantasy story should be an experience for the soul as well as the intellect, emotions, and imagination. By exploring the fantastic, we can learn to see our own world in new ways, to look for the magic of the normal in the real world. It is an Otherness. "Fantasy invokes wonder by making the impossible seem familiar and the familiar seem new and strange."[65]

The realm of fairy-story is wide and deep and high and
filled with many things: all manner of beasts and birds
are found there; shoreless seas and stars uncounted;
beauty that is an enchantment, and an ever present peril;
both joy and sorrow as sharp as swords. In that realm a
man may, perhaps, count himself fortunate to have
wandered but its very richness and strangeness tie the
tongue of a traveler who would report them. And while
he is there it is dangerous for him to ask too many
questions, lest the gates be shut and the keys be lost.[66]

Fantasy is an attempt to fill a hunger and need. Fantasy is a looking back while science fiction is a looking forward. Other than that, and the use of magic versus technology (which is not really that different, depending on the viewpoint used) there is not that much difference between the two, and they should really be seen as one whole genre. The brick-and-mortar bookstores are already doing it. Fantasy has a more 'natural' feel to its wonders. It reaches into the earth and animals, trying to regain what was lost.

Since the Fall ... man has been trying to heal the rift
between himself and ... animals, and to reestablish that
mutual understanding and rapport which he senses must
once have existed and which through the exercise of the

---

[64] J.R.R. Tolkein. *Tree and Leaf.* (Houghton Mifflin Co. Boston 1964) pp. 9-10.
[65] Atteberry. pp. 3.
[66] Tolkein. pp. 3.

literary imagination, if in no other way, might be re-created.⁶⁷

Science fiction/fantasy then stretches minds by putting people in new worlds, with new physical laws, in strange situations they could not meet on Earth. Everything has some parallel in 'reality' and it causes the reader/viewer to think and grow and learn, and perhaps learn about themselves and their world. The really good science fiction/fantasy will hopefully give people the impetus to change the world.

~~~~~

With such a vital force as science fiction/fantasy can be, do Christians dare to leave it solely in the hands of those who only have partial answers, or no answers at all, or who have an agenda to silence believers and mock God's truths? Can Christians let people who do not honor God influence others with their vision of the future and the meaning of life, without offering an enjoyable alternative? Yes, Christians can complain and list what is wrong, but who will really listen? All that anyone hears are complaints. Whining. Criticism. A list of don'ts, but no list of what to do instead. What needs to be done is to make films and books in the same style, with as much color, adventure and quality, and ***something more***. People should be shown what is missing in their lives and hearts and souls. That is the way to change the world, not standing still and screaming while the henhouse burns and foxes steal the chickens.

---

⁶⁷ Swinfen. pp. 12.

MYTH, ALLEGORY, AND MODERN MYTHOLOGY

> Myth is a type of speech ... it is a mode of signification, a form ... Since myth is a type of speech, everything can be a myth provided it is conveyed by a discourse. Myth is not defined by the object of the message, but by the way it utters this message ...[68] (Roland Barthes)

Myth and allegory are far older, more "serious" forms of fantasy. They have a specific teaching purpose to them from the beginning, while science fiction/fantasy is meant to be entertainment from the moment of creation as well as any serious purpose of the author. Through the study of myth and allegory, people can learn about the thoughts and beliefs of ancient peoples. Science fiction/fantasy shows, in general terms, the world views of individuals. But writers today still can use the mythic form to get across their ideas.

> Myth is not an attempt to entertain, it is an attempt to explain something ... they were trying to come to terms with their environment, so you find that over the milenia [sic] myth contains crystallized human experience and very powerful imagery. This imagery is useful for a writer if he uses it responsibly. It can work against him if he does not use it properly, but if he uses it correctly then he has very powerful cutting tools in his hand which work beneath the surface.[69]

While myth is part of history generally, it still applies to today. History can only be studied, to try to prevent disasters from happening again in society, but myth applies to everyone and every time.

> Myth is a story of what <u>happens</u> as distinguished from, but not contradictory to, the history of what <u>has happened</u>. The relationship between myth and history is complementary, in that each is a human vision of events

---

[68] Breen and Corcoran. pp. 127.
[69] Swinfen. pp. 101.

forming a pattern. The patterns of myth are more universal than those of history, their appearance on a deeper level.[70]

Myth is even more a tool of religion than science fiction/fantasy, and hence must be used more carefully so it is not abused and its edge dulled.

Myth is integral to almost every one of man's religions, and particularly to Christianity. Myth is essentially the way man talks about his religious encounter with God and the spiritual world. Eliminate it, and man doesn't have much to talk about religiously; his religion becomes meaningless and flat, or else compulsive.[71]

Just as religion helps people understand a world they cannot see and understand, the workings of the spirit and soul, myth goes a step further and puts those workings into stories they can see and feel. Drama at its very beginning was the acting out of myth to further the ancient people's understanding of the gods and to help them worship. And myth can still be used this way today, as well as drama through stage, TV, and film.

It is this older, more complete understanding of myth to which many perceptive students of mythology are returning. These men, some of them renowned scientists in their own fields, have realized that mythological images refer to a part of reality which cannot be described in ordinary language. Myths, according to these students, are as necessary as the language we use to describe objects and experiences in the outer world. The difference is simply that they speak of another realm of reality and experience, other than the physical one.[72]

Naturally if one does not believe in any such level of reality, then myth becomes something of a puzzle, or even a hindrance to man's effort to get on with the

---

[70] Dabney Adams Hart. *Through the Open Door*. (University of Alabama Press. Birmingham 1984) pp. 13.
[71] Kelsey. pp. 3.
[72] Ibid. pp. 4.

business of clean, sensible, rational, materialistic living. On the other hand, some of the most creative and forward looking scientists have come to the conclusion that scientific discovery itself is not possible without thinking in images and symbols and myths. This has given myth and imagination a new place in men's thinking.[73]

Though myth and allegory are alike in many ways, they are not the same. Myth deals with gods and magic, other lands and worlds and larger-than-life characters. Allegory, like Aesop's fables, deal with ordinary people and things, and animals who stand in for people. They both teach, but allegory is more clearly defined as a teaching vehicle. That is probably why so many shy away from using it: the tendency to grow didactic.

C.S. Lewis says:
My view would be that a good myth (i.e., a story out of which ever varying meanings will grow for different readers and in different ages) is a higher thing than allegory (into which <u>one</u> meaning has been put). Into an allegory a man can put only what he already knows: in a myth he puts what he does not yet know and could not come by any other way.[74]

Allegory can be a myth or any kind of story. One of the meanings associated with allegory is the term <u>hyponoia</u>, which is "the hidden, underlying meaning of a story or myth, or a conjecture or guess about such a meaning."[75]

The significant elements in ancient thought relating to allegory or possibly relating to allegory, include: 1) otherspeaking (by similarity or contrast); 2) a succession of metaphors; 3) seven species -- irony, antiphasis, riddle, chorientismos, astismos, sarcasm, and proverb or proverb and application; 4) visualizing and concretizing the invisible and abstract; 5) symbolic gods and events; 6) personifications; 7) allusion; 8) literal, external

---

[73] Ibid. pp. 5.
[74] Timmerman. pp. 7.
[75] Phillip Rollinson. *Classical Theories of Allegory and Christian Culture.* (Duquesne University Press. Pittsburgh 1981) pp. 3.

concealment of a hidden, inner meaning; 9) fable as impossible story; 10) concealed biographical reference; and 11) analogy as comparison, parable, example and fable. Clearly these elements are all interrelated and in some cases subordinated to each other.[76]

When the word 'mythology' is mentioned, a majority of people think of Greco/Roman and Norse myths, which they were taught in school. Unless the family had a strong ethnic heritage, kept alive by costumes, special holidays, storytelling, etc., the individual might not be aware of other cultural mythologies. Each nation has them: Incans, Aztecs, American Indians, Ancient Britons, Germans, Australian Bushmen, etc.

At first glance, it seems that except for classical myths studied in school, the Modern American has no mythology. If that is true, they are in trouble, for myth fills a vital function in emotional, mental, and spiritual health. (Some might offer folk tales as modern mythology, and they would have a point, but I'm referring to the mythology that answers questions about life.) But America today does have its own mythology, tailored to fit its needs, style, and tastes. It is called science fiction and fantasy.

First, mythology must be more clearly defined before it can be determined if the genre fits the pattern. Myth is defined by what it does.

... myth is a body of narratives woven into a culture which dictates belief, defines ritual, and acts as a chart of the social order.[77]

Myth functions, first, as part of the perceptual system of a culture through which unfamiliar situations originating either within the culture or outside it, are interpreted and fitted into old symbolic molds ... In helping to pattern the relationships among basic beliefs, values, and behaviors that organize social interaction, myths produce common social understandings of new social conditions.[78]

---

[76] Ibid. pp. 18.
[77] Breen. pp. 128.
[78] Ibid. pp. 128.

For example, a tribe finds its food source dwindling, and because of taboos, cannot turn to a more available source. The holy man, after much thought, prayer, reading signs and considering his dreams, would come up with permission to use the other food source, as well as an explanation why the shortage had come about. The next time this happened, the people would have precedent to fall back on and help them understand what was going on and what to do.

A second function of myth is to create exemplary models for a whole society in process that translates a single life-history into an archetype, thereby setting up patterns for imitation ... the screen media play a similar role in setting up heroes and heroines to carry on mythological traditions.[79]

The hope, the anticipation of fantasy and mythic literature is that by bringing a power larger than men but apparent through men to bear upon this world, we can once again kindle the light of the human spirit. The nature of that power ... is constituted of enduring and indomitable values such as heroism, chivalry, a sense of good over against evil.[80]

Examples of this second function would be heroes like Hercules, Theseus, Ulysses, Odin, Thor, Beowulf, Kon-Tiki and Quetzalcoatl. These people were the ideals of strength, wisdom, cunning, compassion, and bravery for their people. Because they were ideals they were also too good to be true, too perfect to be all in one man. Likely each of these heroes had a basis in fact. Perhaps they were combinations of the characteristics and exploits of a number of men, melded together into one after a great deal of time had passed.

But the legends, the myths, were preserved because they had something to say and show to the people of the cultures they belonged to. The heroes were held up to all the following generations as a goal to strive for, an example to measure their own

---

[79] Ibid. pp. 129.
[80] Timmerman. pp. 28.

exploits, behaviors and gifts against. With a goal, something to compare themselves to, people try harder. Runners make better time when they race against people, not just the stopwatch. Competition, even against ancient people, makes others work harder and achieve more.

> A third major function of myth is the power it gives for handling conflicts, both within a culture itself and between cultures. When alternative forms of social organization present themselves, myth is a language of argument, not a chorus of harmony.[81]

If a people's beliefs and goals are recorded in some form that shows them how these beliefs and goals function, how easy will it be for them to be shaken? With examples of other people facing similar difficulties by following certain rules, a person can withstand conflicts much longer than without. Knowing that others succeeded before will give a person confidence to endure.

And by the same token, knowing that such beliefs work and bring positive results, the person who holds them will hold onto them much longer against new beliefs, especially if the second contradicts the first. The known, the tried and proven, is much more certain than new and/or contradictory. Thus, while it may make conflicts stronger, myth helps cultures stay more stable.

Also, when cultural beliefs conflict, myth helps to define when contradictory rules apply so that they no longer oppose each other. Take violence and killing, for example. "A fundamental need of our mythology has been to conceal the homogeneity of violent acts, to support the difference between 'good' or beneficial violence, and 'evil' or destructive violence, and to justify the former."[82] Myth will show that fighting to defend oneself is a good type of violence. Defending others is better, and acting as a soldier in war is the best, most honorable thing of all. Yet the same culture also has rules that say killing and violence are dishonorable things. Myth will show that bad violence is when a person kills for gain, malice, in defense of evil, or when directed against innocent and helpless people. Myth

---

[81] Breen. pp. 130.
[82] Tyrell. pp. 290.

smooths out conflicts within a culture and helps it stand during conflict with other cultures and their values.

> A fourth function of myth is the reduction of the continuous randomness of historical experience to an intelligible pattern ... Myths, therefore, function as part of the reification of a culture, that is, they are part of the cultural construction of the reality of that culture.[83]

In the same way that myth combines several great men into an ideal, a hero, myth also may put several historical incidents into one big battle or journey, so that the impact is greater and it is more beautiful and memorable. The things that are important to the society or culture are preserved, lifted up and altered to suit the needs of the time. In essence, the rock of history is pounded apart, the gems and valuable minerals extracted, and the useless slag and dust discarded.

> The Fantastic or Mythical is a mode available at all ages ... If it is well used by the author and meets the right reader it has the same power: to generalize while remaining concrete, to present in palpable form not concepts or even experiences but whole classes of experience, and to throw off irrelevancies. But at its best it can do more; it can give us experiences we have never had and then, instead of 'commenting on life,' can add to it.[84]

Myth expands the images of the mind by educating the hearer about the rest of the world, other cultures, and history. By giving the hearers vicarious experiences they would not otherwise go through, myth helps in the growth of personality. It teaches, touching the soul, whether in a conscious or unconscious way.

Myth can be a story about anthropomorphized creatures and superior people or gods. But myth is more than just story. Myth uses symbol and allegory to accomplish its multiple duties. Without these two elements, myth would just be a story to entertain and pass on tradition or history, but nothing beyond or deeper in meaning.

---

[83] Breen. pp. 131.
[84] Hooper. pp. 48.

> ... a fabric of symbolism may enable the writer to create a moral and intellectual framework for the action of his novel. Symbolism allows an author to link the limited world of his characters to one of the great systems of values, so that we are made to compare the happenings of the novel with the mythological or historical parallels. Specific actions in the story illustrate general patterns of behavior, and the private character acquires a new importance when he is seen in the light of his symbolic counterpart.[85]

For example, the River Styx in Greco/Roman myth was a symbol for the experience of death. It was the cold, bitter barrier, sometimes violent and painful, between life and death. Symbol is a concrete thing standing for an idea or event or concept too great to be fully comprehended, which may then require multiple symbols or metaphors. For example, Jesus is a shepherd as well as a lamb, a lion, a wall, a door, a child, a dove. Limiting Him to one metaphor would be denying part of the vast, near-incomprehensible aspect of Him. In another vein, Jesus is none of these things, yet they can stand for Him. "Remember that symbol is a way of expressing truth -- it does not denote something that is not true."[86]

As for allegory, many can be contained within one myth. Allegory "is the hidden, underlying meaning in a story or myth, or a conjecture or guess about such a meaning."[87] Allegory, if handled carefully, can mean something different for each person who reads it. When allegory is blatantly obvious, it can only mean one thing, no matter how many people look at it. For example, *Pilgrim's Progress* would need much twisting and turning and rewriting for people to get a different sermon from it than what John Bunyan meant. Myth, on the other hand, depends for its interpretation on the mental, emotional, and spiritual background of the reader or hearer. For example, where one person reading the *Odyssey* of Homer today would only see an adventure story, another would see a tale of enduring love, and a third reader would obtain a view of the Greek

---

[85] Tolkein. pp. 100.
[86] Lee A. Belford. Editor. *Religious Dimensions in Literature*. (Seabury Press. NY 1982) pp. 14.
[87] Rollinson. pp. 3.

society and manners of that period, and yet another would come away with a tale of man's triumph over adversity by using his mind and living a life approved of by the gods. And all the readers would learn from the experience.

One important theme in myth concerns the activities of the gods, their relationships with each other, the world, and humans. None of them are inactive. They are either for or against the mortal characters, never neutral. Why? Because humans needed to know, to understand, to somehow capture the gods for study. People had to find some way to gain the help of the gods, avoid their anger, or appease their wrath. People could not survive without the gods, because they sensed there was much to life that was beyond their senses to understand and beyond their powers to affect. Religion is the attempt to understand the world beyond the one known by humans, and understand its inhabitants as well.

Myth essentially invokes a sense of awe, wonder, mystery and beauty. Perhaps myth seems to have died out in the Christianized world because the Church has lost a large portion of that sense of awe, etc. Rationality is such an important issue that any sense of mystery in the Church is ignored, either because nothing can solve that mystery, or because someone claims to have solved it. This could also explain the upsurge in the Pentecostal movement: people are hungry for awe, mystery, and wonder in their worship. They need to have some elements of religious life that cannot be explained clearly and concretely, but only sensed and hinted at. A return to myth and mythic elements in the Church would satisfy that hunger and need. The Pentecostal movement fills much of the lack, but it tends towards emotionalism and individualism too much in the experience, in my opinion. Myth is the mystical that can be shared, recorded, and passed on so others may recapture the experience.

> The present interest in myth reflects a need and search for order and certainty in the midst of the apparent chaos and disorder of the 20th century.[88]

Numerous philosophies have attempted to kill the interest in myth and nullify the effect it has on people's lives. Humanism claims all Humanity's answers come from within, not from outside

---

[88] Timmerman. pp. 21.

sources. Philosophies of rationalism and elitism denigrate myth as old-fashioned, something that interferes with logic and the proper function of the intellect. Myth and fantasy became unfashionable. But the need remained, so it resurrected in new, fashionable forms. Science fiction/fantasy tends to the future, to technology, Humanity bettering itself, to satisfy the new philosophers, as well as a touch of romance and daring. But it also fills the mythic functions of explaining, giving examples, exciting wonder and awe, and resolving conflicts. Use of the imagination, thinking in intangibles, is necessary for solving problems and invention in the modern world, which many people have at last discovered and acknowledged.

> Myths are narratives with the power to explain something in our world: e.g., why the hyacinth is purple, why we must work for a living, or why death is a beginning, not an end. Myths define an image of the world within and without and relate us to it emotionally. They put in narrative form the unconscious assumptions and anxieties of a culture. They elaborate and justify the former; the latter they circumvent or camouflage. The result is integration of self and self with the cosmos. During the 60s American myths and the values they supported increasingly failed to address the contemporary consciousness. Star Trek recreated their power to explain by displacing them into a futuristic, quasi-scientific setting.[89]

Star Trek appeared at a time when the United States was beginning to sink in hopelessness. The old ideals were being questioned. Role models were no longer applicable to the situation. Beliefs contradicted each other. Star Trek, and most of the science fiction/fantasy that has followed in its wake, suddenly gave back heroes, ideals, and clear-cut solutions. When people were worried that computers would take away the need for their minds, and automation would steal jobs, Capt. Kirk defeated computers right and left, overcoming superior minds and resources with human stubbornness and ingenuity.

---

[89] Tyrell. pp. 288.

> Fear of being outmoded or replaced by a machine has accompanied the rise of automation. Although machines have improved the general welfare and led to the so-called 'leisure age,' for many it has been at the price of the dignity of work ... Computers in particular cause such anxieties because they are readily anthropomorphized.[90]
>
> The myth of the computer deals with anthropomorphization, replacement, machine intelligence, and free will.[91]

When people worried about the rightness of fighting, even when it was for what they strongly believed in, the crew of the *Enterprise* showed how to handle the battle with clear consciences and a happy ending for everyone.

> The crux of the motif is the projection of communal fears, such as nuclear holocaust or the possibility of a cataclysmic accident, upon a monster, which is then slain by society's champion. In this way tension within society is relieved without having to admit that its source is society itself.[92]

Star Trek helped people by reinforcing beliefs that the human race is superior and will always remain superior, against aliens, foreign technology and science, and its own creations. Star Trek showed that Humanity will grow wiser, yet not change in terms of values, affections, and goals.[93] And Star Trek promised that there would always be some kind of answer, no matter how difficult and ambiguous the question.

> Every effect in its cosmos has a cause and is fully comprehensible in terms of that cause. 'I want some answers, Mister,' Kirk demands and he gets them. There is no area left to chance; nothing is unknown ... But causality functions as a myth; it is a story that Star Trek tells to affirm that there is nothing new or strange

---

[90] Ibid. pp. 289
[91] Ibid. pp. 289.
[92] Ibid. pp. 288.
[93] Ibid. pp. 288.

> anywhere around us. Inherent in the universe, however, is a purpose. Although Star Trek admits no change in man's physical makeup, he is advancing toward a better rendition of himself.[94]
>
> Man, the product of natural selection, will continue to evolve morally in those qualities that make for perfection of his species. Like causality, this is a mythic view because it uses a biological concept to answer non-biological questions. What is good for man, for instance, is a philosophical or metaphysical question, and is not subject to the rigorous demonstration and proof of science.[95]

Science fiction/fantasy touches all areas of life and time. It touches the mind and emotions, brain and spirit, individual and society. And this is what myth does. Modern people have no vital mythology as did the Greeks.

> The supremacy of the Judeo-Christian philosophy in western people's lives is not what it once was. The authority of science fiction as myth exists in its roots in modern science. In the absence of myth or religion, people have instead found solace in fictional science that paints unknown futures where exist the imagined achievement of their waking dreams. And science fiction does fulfill a function one associates with myth: it fills the reader with a sense of wonder and awe. Its confines are the past, the present, and the future, its base is science, its premise is 'what if,' and its path, the path of imagination.[96]

Returning to the quote from George Lucas, myth and fairy tales prepare the young to take their place in society. If parents don't tell their children fairy tales, and the Church doesn't supply the role

---

[94] Ibid. pp. 293.
[95] Ibid. pp. 294.
[96] John Aquino. *Science Fiction as Literature*. pp. 21.

models and mythical training, where will children get this necessary information? From science fiction/fantasy.[97]

Science fiction/fantasy is the form which myth has taken in modern society. The physical boundaries are expanded and the character titles are changed, but the basic structure, intent, and effects are still the same. Instead of being set on Earth in the present or past, the stories are also on other worlds, in other galaxies and times. With so much of Earth's geography known, and historical records so readily available, some of the suspension of disbelief in myth is harder to come by. Set the story in a world and time unknown, and it is suddenly much more believable and hence able to get its point across much more easily. The characters themselves, whether aliens, robots, or humans, can trace their "roots" back to types of heroes, people with god-like powers, and dilemmas, in ancient myth.

Perhaps one of the reasons science fiction/fantasy is not recognized as myth is because people have the conception that myth is ancient, simplistic, and primitive. The attempts of myth to explain the inexplicable are very clear to readers now. Just how simplistic will today's science fiction/fantasy/mythology seem to people hundreds of years from now, and how easily will they see through the attempts at explanation and preparation? Remember, as knowledge increases and boundaries expand, myth moves with them.

The religious elements of science fiction/fantasy have been discussed elsewhere, and will not be delved into here, other than to say that as myth fulfills a religious function, so does science fiction/fantasy.

Only a few examples of science fiction/fantasy will be discussed here in terms of its mythic parallels. Because of George Lucas' beliefs on the teaching value of the genre, *Return of the Jedi* is a prime example.

> One of the reasons *Return of the Jedi* is so popular is that it contains a clear-cut series of oppositions that give it meaning. Thus, we find the following oppositions in the story: Youth/Old age. Luke/The Emperor. Nature/Technology. Forest/Death Star. The Force/Evil.

---

[97] Short. pp. 49.

The Rebels/The Empire. Freedom/Tyranny. Love/Hate. Good Beasts/Bad Beasts. Ewoks/Jabba's army. The Son/The Father. These oppositions help make the fairy tale understandable to viewers and provide them with easy objects to identify with or despise.[98]

People are able to see by their actions who is good and who evil. The good win, not without sacrifice and pain, thus encouraging people to choose good over evil, and hold on through bad times. Everything is clear, even as it is entertaining. It gives hope and a goal to reach to, for the viewer who takes the movie's inherent message to heart.

A good deal of science fiction/fantasy deals with the quest motif. A hero must make a journey, spiritual, emotional and /or physical, for the purpose of rescuing others, or to satisfy a hunger or need within himself. Through the hero's travels and lessons, the reader of the story travels and learns as well. Star Trek handled this quest theme well, as the whole crew learned and battled for the good of the Federation and each other. Star Trek is ...

... the archetype of the hero with a thousand faces: only by striving towards the unknown, by surmounting danger, does the individual win his identity. To deny or refuse that quest is to remain one with the herd. At a time when the individual feels reduced to a number, Star Trek's recreation of the heroic archetype is especially appealing.[99]

Returning to the theme of justifying certain types of violence and defining which is good and which bad, Star Trek tackles the problem quite often. One episode in particular stated the problem and solution/rationalization. *The Savage Curtain* had Spock and Kirk teamed with recreations of two great men of peace from the past of Earth and Vulcan, Abraham Lincoln and Surak, respectively. They had to battle with villains from the past of other planets, held captive on the planet Excalbia by omnipotent-seeming creatures. These captors merely wanted to learn about good and evil and see

---

[98] Berger. pp. 73.
[99] Tyrell. pp. 290.

which was stronger. If the good side won, the *Enterprise* would be set free. If evil conquered, the recreations of evil would be allowed to live again and roam the galaxy. Both sides used the same tactics, and (naturally) the good won. When asked how they could claim to be good when they fought just as evil did, Kirk made it clear he only fought because he had to, to save the lives and freedom of others. Thus, violence to help others, and not for personal gain, is good.

> Yet Americans decry violence and have developed the motif of redemptive violence to justify its use ... Accordingly, the men of the *Enterprise* undergo suffering to redeem a damsel from oppression, or a people from substandard ways, thereby reassuring themselves of the worth of their culture and goals. But the redemptive motif is subordinated to another purpose. Redemption is the means by which the myths, whether Star Trek's myth of science or that of America as World Savior, hide from believers the realization that their violence is identical to that of their enemy.[100]

Writers in the genre use mythic ways to express the questions and problems of the age. Some insist that all science fiction writing should be based on real, scientific fact and possibility; many writers use a little fact and extrapolate on it to serve as a base for their mythical intentions. "Science fiction qualifies as the most interesting example of deliberate intervention in the usually hidden cultural mechanism which generates myth."[101]

What are the implications of this switchover of labels? When the toys and costumes are stripped away, and myth and science fiction/fantasy are taken down to their basics, they are much alike. Both function in and affect society in the same way. They reflect Humanity's views of the universe and all realms of time and space, it must be remembered. They present glimpses and hints of truth, and interpretation varies from person to person, depending on each one's background. Both myth and science fiction/fantasy have a potential for strong effects on society, reinforcing values or bringing about

---

[100] Ibid. pp. 290.
[101] Breen. pp. 135.

change. For this reason, they must be used with care, and not left to be tools of the opposition.

"RELIGIOUS" vs. "CHRISTIAN"

> We may profit from the illuminations and stimulations of conjecture. We may take insight and strength from imaginative events and symbols that dramatize for us doctrinal abstractions (remember that Jesus Himself never dealt in theological abstractions but always in parable and act). But we must remember the fallibility and inadequacy of human imagination and symbols.[102]
> (Edmund Fuller)

Anything creative made by humans depends a great deal on the interpretation of both artist and consumer for the impact of the message contained therein. No two people can possibly have the same life experiences and reactions, beliefs, attitudes, tastes, etc. All of this will affect how they interpret the symbolism in the books or films they experience. Some will gain more understanding than others. One person will see evil while the people to the right and left will see images of God in the exact same things. Therefore, the interpretation of anything is personal and will differ, even if only in miniscule ways, from person to person. At the same time, there can be much agreement because of shared beliefs.

Remember all the varied descriptions of science fiction/fantasy. Consider this thought: "SF is predominantly speculative, looking forward and outward. Fantasy is more introspective and traditional: it attempts to revivify old metaphors and reembody old mythologies."[103] Science fiction/fantasy then stretches the mind by putting the reader into a new world, with new physical laws, in strange situations that could not be met on Earth. Everything has some sort of parallel in reality and provides the reader-viewer the opportunity to think and grow and learn.

At this point, some people might protest it is all evil because the genre does not follow natural laws. Science fiction/fantasy is an *extrapolation* of this world into another. The really good, worthwhile stories are the ones containing realistic people, like the

---

[102] Belford. Editor. pp. 12.
[103] Atteberry. pp. 26-27.

ones in the real world, emotionally, mentally, and intellectually, if not physically, socially, etc. By putting ordinary people into settings and situations that are not normal, it is sometimes easier to observe the way people are, and learn from it. The author and consumer both agree that the world is not real, but that does not mean they cannot explore it and use what they learn.

Writers in the genre can't help but apply their own world views, their philosophies, beliefs, ideals, etc. to the worlds they create. In reading the stories or viewing the films, the audience picks up on these things. They may then apply some to their own lives. This system of beliefs, etc., can be called 'religious.'

> Space fantasy, or 'science fiction' may never even mention anything 'religious' in the ordinary sense of the word. But whenever this fiction tries to help people find ultimate meaning for their lives, then it is -- by definition -- <u>religious</u>. As a religious fiction it will often display very sensitive and accurate intuition of what all people are basically hungering and thirsting for. And insofar as it understands *Christ* as the answer to this hunger and thirst, then it's an expression of the *Christian* 'religion.' But even when this fiction <u>doesn't</u> understand Christ as the fulfillment of these needs, it still can bear an unintentional, unconscious, almost predictable resemblance to Christ. Just because of the genuineness, the sincerity, and the forcefulness of the questions behind it.[104]

Religious science fiction/fantasy is literature that tries to find and give answers. There are a lot of questions being asked in the world, and even if there is only a hint of some kind of answer in the genre, no wonder it is so popular. But why are so many turning to it instead of to more traditional sources? As George Lucas stated:

> ... there was no contemporary fairy tales ... the number of parents who sit down and tell their children fairy tales is dwindling. As families begin to break up, kids are left more to the television ... As a result, people are learning their mythology from TV, which makes them very

---

[104] Short. pp. 15.

confused because it has no point of view, no sense of morality ... unless a child has a very strong family life or is involved with the church, there's no anchor to hold on to ... It's where religion comes from. Fairy tales, religion, were all designed to teach man the right way to live and give him a moral anchor.[105]

Certainly the life ideals and role models shown in movies and books are much more appealing than the list of rules and dry lectures many churches provide. "The fact remains that films like *Close Encounters* ... have become jerrybuilt substitutes for the great myths and rituals of belief, hope and redemption ... "[106] The modern mythology of science fiction/fantasy can do a great deal of good for the world today.

> ... the moral aspect of the stories is of significant importance. Stories of this type, based as they are on praise of honesty, cordiality, bravery, manliness, tolerance, fellow-feeling, support of the deprived, encounter with the oppressor and such other moral virtues could go a long way to neutralize the undesirable influences of ... Civilization. They would at the same time create a repugnance and a capacity for resistance against selfishness, exploitation, unconcern for others, violence, promiscuity and similar other evils of the machine age.[107]

Religious science fiction/fantasy contains a very broad list of philosophies, ideals, religions, etc. -- from Neitzche to Confucius, Eastern thought and Judeo-Christian beliefs. What sets Christian works apart from the merely religious? It has been suggested that the author makes the story Christian if he is a Christian. This idea infers that the author's world view enters the story without any conscious effort on his part. That is a good criteria, but is it the only one? Sometimes a story written by a Christian author has no identifiable characteristics of his beliefs until a good deal of thinking and

---

[105] Ibid. pp. 49.
[106] Ibid. pp. 15.
[107] Heinz-Dietrich Fischer, PhD. and Stefan Reinhard Melnik, MA. Editors. *Entertainment: A Cross-Cultural Examination.* (Hastings House Publishers. NY 1979) pp. 60.

research has been done on the part of the reader. Unless the readers are theologians or are looking for the Christian significance, will they find it? Discovery could be dependent upon knowing the author is Christian, and knowing what Christianity means. For example, someone could read ***The Hobbit*** and the Lord of the Rings series, not knowing J.R.R. Tolkein was a Christian, find this fact out later, and upon reading the four books again, see the Christian parallels.

Is the story Christian if it shows parallels to Christ in its characters and actions? Must these parallels be sharply defined, or only shadows, loosely defined as such? If only a few elements in the story can be called Christian, is the whole story Christian by association? This would make the Dune books and the Star Wars movies Christian because of the few Christian elements woven into the Eastern influences. This cannot be allowed. With all the unconscious parallels to Christianity in other religions, if this rule were followed, *all* religions could be called Christian. Therefore, a Christian science fiction/fantasy story must follow the core Christian doctrines in the main actions and ideologies espoused. That gives a lot of leeway in the props and costuming and set design. For instance, I have a long-term project waiting that is essentially the Incarnation (God taking on Human flesh) set on a world ship, but the Christ figure is female ... I'm sure some will accuse me of blasphemy, and while others will proclaim me a prophet of a new Reformation ... I just want to tell the core story of Redemption from a new angle. And science-fiction/fantasy allows that! (Someday, I promise, I will get the book written. Look for ***Tabairna*** ... someday!)

Enough meandering. Back to the topic:

So, there are two criteria so far for separating Christian science fiction/fantasy from the merely religious. First, the author must be Christian. Second, the beliefs, doctrines, etc. espoused or taught by example must all follow basic Christian doctrines.

What follows is a discussion of a few movies and books to discern whether they are Christian or merely religious. *Close Encounters* comes first.

> There are three dominant scenes in *Close Encounters* and each says something about the nature of American religion ... One is the scene where the Dreyfuss character is exposed to the power of the extraterrestrial beings. His

truck is apparently held in a force-field; his face is burnt by a strong light; a traffic-sign wobbles like a limber tree branch; the contents of his glove compartment are scattered and torn, and then returned, whole and unscathed. This scene shows the religious force has utter command over the material world, but is fundamentally uninterested in it ...

The second scene of great force in the movie is where the child, a three-year-old named Barry ... is drawn out by the uncanny display of the spaceship, only to return unharmed. The child is made to appear beatific in this scene, and the implication is that the higher 'adult' power is at heart childlike and innocent.

The third stunning scene opens the movie; it shows a squadron of fighter-planes, lost for some years, returned in perfect order, untouched and unaffected by the passage of time. Again, the theme of an otherworldly but harmless power is manifest.[108]

... *Close Encounters* rests on an unexamined belief that there can be a new, post-Christian, post- transcendent religion in America. This new religion, in many ways, is a new version of man, and is thus a secular religion ... This post-Enlightenment view of religion is both replenished and modified by *Close Encounters.* This contemporary religion senses that the sacred is *'of this world,'* but not *'in* this world,' to rephrase the New Testament formulation. The new religious force, incarnated in Spielberg's extraterrestrial curators, is out of this world in one sense, but clearly in the solar system in another sense. The 'invaders' are less intruding beings from elsewhere than they are tender, even solicitous caretakers, intent only on studying certain specimens of our species, as if engaged in 'quality control.'[109]

---

[108] Molesworth. pp. 262-263.
[109] Ibid. pp. 261.

This movie hints at a Supreme being, but one that merely set the world going. He doesn't care about his creation, except to check in from time to time for quality control. Perhaps the closest Spielberg comes to hitting the mark is when the aliens are 'childlike,' so that the young and innocent feel no fear during their encounters with the beings. Spielberg, like many other Americans, rewrites religions to suit the view he has of the universe. A creator who doesn't really care frees people of the obligation to follow rules.

Probably the most furor aroused by the genre in religious circles (aside from Harry Potter) was over the Star Wars movies. Quite frankly, the fault is with the Christians, not George Lucas. There is something wrong expecting non-Christian movie makers and writers to produce works in exact accordance with Christian doctrine. Christians saw a few elements parallel with their theology, and expected the whole movie to be purely Christian. When they didn't get what they wanted, instead of admitting they were wrong, they ripped apart the film and its creator. The Star Wars movies concern the everlasting battle between good and evil. The Force, which is the center of the controversy, is not the God of Judeo-Christian belief, but perhaps Humanity's potential, talent, and personal power. The dark side of the Force is the potential for evil; it is strength of will. It is all those things, as well as being the 'life force' as described by Obi Wan Kenobi. The Star Wars universe is not Christian, though it might have a few aspects of Christianity. But it is religious. People can base their lives and philosophies on the dark or light side of the Force, and decide which side of the battle between good and evil they will fight on.

One of the most popular universes in the genre is the ever-expanding world of Star Trek. With movies in the Classic Trek, Next Generation and the reboot series, plus multiple TV series and an animated series, in syndication all over the world, clubs, role-playing games, conventions, and by now probably hundreds of books all centered around this one creation of Gene Roddenberry, there must be something that draws people to it. Some of it is the hope, philosophies, and examples presented in the stories. The *Enterprise* is crewed by a mixture of people representing all races, worlds, and politics, working together in harmony. They are a peaceful military, searching for knowledge to profit and improve everyone. They work for the United Federation of Planets, a large group of voluntary members. This is about as close to utopia as most universes can get without offending someone because of a note of unreality of restraints on freedom. The Federation has problems internally, and it has enemies, but there is always hope that these problems will be solved, and that someday, the enemies will become friends. There is a possibility for peace and prosperity for everyone. The future, according to Star Trek, will be one of peace and plenty, where Earth will have overcome all its prejudices and differences, so the larger problems can be attacked.

Despite all its beauty, there are flaws in Trek's philosophy. All this progress is brought about through the *will* of humans. People did it, on their own, in their own power, with superior technology. The knowledge is increased, but spirit and soul haven't changed. Success is brought about by mutual interdependence, but there is no dependance on any power *greater* than Humanity. Once in a while, references are made to some higher power, but while the crew of the *Enterprise* is aware of Someone out there, they do what's right because it's what they believe, not because God (or whatever higher power they bow to) says so. They give good examples for living, they have high morals, but they aren't the perfect example of Jesus. Except perhaps for Mr. Spock, who finds all manner of evil totally illogical. Yet even he will resort to lying, violence, and stealing if it is necessary. "Spock is the Christ figure in that he is the mediator between the everyday world -- ours and that of the Enterprise -- and a wonderland of infinite possibility ... He stands between what we know and what we deem knowable with aid. He is the way, our guide in the heroic struggle for identity."[110]

The world of Dune, created by Frank Herbert, has books written by other authors, games, and multiple versions of the first novel. I will discuss only the first three books in the series because those are the only ones I've read. The books are blatantly religious. There are many different religious groups and beliefs discussed through the stories. Paul, the main character, is a messianic figure, foretold long ago. But though there are parallels to a Christ figure, the stories are not Christian. There is no referral to a higher power. All power, all decisions of right and wrong, rest in people's own

---

[110] Tyrell. pp. 295.

consciences, in the philosophies made up by men. (And every man did what was right in his own sight ...) Certainly the depraved and evil are overthrown, but there is no real proof that the people who succeed them are spiritually superior to them, only morally and aesthetically. The world of Dune presents interesting philosophies, but none concurrent with those of Christ. Its philosophies can be lived by, somewhat, but there is nothing to nourish the soul or save it.

The Dragonriders of Pern series, by Anne McCaffrey, lacks any sense of religion or allegiance to a higher power in the lives of her characters. (I have read a few references to her dislike for "organized religion," and her irritation when a fan insisted there had to be some religious element to her society. I have to wonder if she was hurt by someone who was religious, but definitely not a follower of Christ. Doesn't it amaze you sometimes, so many people who say they are Christians, but ignore most of what Jesus said?) Her characters live and do their best, and are highly moral and responsible, but they only answer to themselves and the authorities among them. There is no mention of an afterlife or spiritual realm. But her people are so real, so believable, that the reader never notices the lack while reading. It is interesting that the morals are for the most part highly Christian -- the people who harm others get their just desserts, often at their own hands. The characters are good people, and if that was all there was necessary to live life and be happy, fine. But that isn't all.

One element of the dragon/rider relationship has very spiritual overtones. When the dragons hatch, a psychic link is formed, called Impression, between dragon and rider. It is akin to Vulcan bonding (if that is any help). Dragon and rider are always together, in spirit and mind. The human is never alone, never lacks someone who understands perfectly. It is close to what marriage should be. But also, it is an allegory for what the Christian's relationship with God can be -- God is always present, always in perfect communication and rapport and understanding. Christians *are* never alone, but how often are they aware of it?

Just from this shallow survey, one large element that sets *religious* science fiction/fantasy apart from *Christian* is the lack of awareness of a higher power. Power, strength, wisdom, talents, and victory come through a person's own efforts, not as gifts from another. Therefore, it can be safely said that a third criteria of Christian writing in the genre is recognition of a person/wisdom/power beyond Humankind, to whom they are responsible and answerable. And not just an impersonal force, but one that is just, wise, loving, merciful and personal.

J.R.R. Tolkein's four books about Hobbits are based in a realm and time called Middle Earth. Readers only see a small corner of this creation. In the book ***The Silmarillion***, this world is created. The Creator is seen and heard as He works. One of His high servants falls. In many of the events, the reader can see parallels between Middle Earth and the Bible. First, the enemy is one who had great power and let it seduce him to evil, instead of using it for others as intended. His evil drew the rest of the land into misery, and his influence caused others to fall. Gandalf, the wizard, is a servant of good. He uses his wisdom to help others, not for gain. At one point in the story, he loses his life for the others in his group and is reborn after going through fire and ice, from the deepest depths (Hell) to the highest heights (Heaven). He is no longer Gandalf the Grey, but Gandalf the White. He is stronger and wiser, and the things of the world and past are no longer of paramount concern to him. He is eager and willing to help the good even more. Gandalf knows his power comes not from himself, so he is not proud.

The next books more blatantly acknowledge a God-figure. It doesn't matter what He is called, whether Aslan, Maleldil, or the Most High, for He is always recognizable as God and Jesus Christ. His actions, laws, and words do not contradict what the Bible teaches.

In the Chronicles of Narnia and the Space Trilogy of C.S. Lewis, Jesus is called Aslan and Maleldil, respectively. Aslan is shown sacrificing His life for a sinner. On the planets Malacandra and Perelandra, Ransom tells others of what Maleldil has already done in coming to Earth and giving His life. The main characters must set to right what is wrong, drawn from their worlds into new ones, with new physical laws and mythologies. And these people cannot set things right under their own powers. They must rely on the strength and guiding of Aslan or Maleldil. It doesn't matter how unreal or unearthly or magical the creatures of this new world are, they have souls that need saving and lives that need rescuing and reordering. God is the same for all of them.

In the Dragon King Trilogy, by Steve Lawhead, the main characters are born into the world where they have their adventure. It is unclear if the Messiah has come in this world, or is still to come. The only information the people have about God Most High, in a land full of temples and impersonal deities, comes from the books and records of a vanished people. Quentin is the first main character, and the three books follow him from adolescence to maturity as husband and father. He takes a spiritual journey as he learns to obey and believe in the God Most High. He parallels the problems, blessings, and miracles of Christians in general as they learn to serve Jesus Christ.

... success in sacred literature depends on the same qualities of structure, suspense, variety, diction, and the like which secure success in secular literature.[111] (C.S. Lewis)

Yet it isn't just being Christian that will make a science fiction/fantasy story good. So much of what I read in high school and college that tried to pass for Christian work in the genre often struck me as infantile, contrived, blatant, didactic, or some combination of the four. A lot of people had the same attitude toward Christian fiction that people in my church had toward doing drama. Ever heard the reference to "bathrobe drama" in churches? I remember one year one of the shepherds for the Christmas pageant showed up in a robe that had fire trucks on it. His costumer (his mother), when asked to provide a robe that looked more realistic for the time (meaning stripes or a solid color) responded, "Oh, well, it's just for the church. Nobody will care." Umm, excuse me? If you're doing it for the church, meaning you're doing it for God, shouldn't you put forth your best effort? Shouldn't you make sure every detail is as close to perfect as it can be? Saying it's "just" for the church implies that your audience doesn't deserve the best storytelling you can provide.

Whew, sorry about that rant, but ... it needs to be said. It needed to be said forty years ago!

Luckily, the amount of good work for Christians is growing by leaps and bounds, thanks to organizations such as Realm Makers

---

[111] C.S. Lewis. *Christian Reflections*. pp. 23.

and the Speculative Fiction chapter of American Christian Fiction Writers, and other organizations of believers who love fantastic worlds and otherworldly storytelling. However, keep in mind: *some concepts and ideas are not meant to be expressed in science fiction/fantasy. The medium must be compatible to the message. The sender must also be comfortable with the medium, or it will not work.*

> C.S. Lewis once wrote in a letter:
> I turned to fairy tales because that seemed the form which certain ideas and images in my mind seemed to demand; as a man might turn to fugues because the musical phrases in his head seemed to him to be 'good fugal subjects.'[112]

For the Christian working in science fiction/fantasy, care must be taken with the symbolism used. A balance must be maintained between vagueness and blatancy. There are some people who will insist on misunderstanding everything they read, and will see evil in a symbol the writer uses for good. Often this is a result of the reader's warped worldview, but care must be taken anyway. Christian writers must make clear what the symbols and metaphors mean, without being didactic and killing the fun of the story, or being too obvious with the message. Theater majors are always told, "If you want to send a message, use Western Union." As a Christian, the writer's worldview will come through even when it isn't done consciously. The main idea is to explore the story, the conflicts and feelings and actions, and let the story tell itself. The "message," if there is supposed to be one, will come through.

The genre is a wide open field for Christian writers. With the Church no longer a common part of most people's upbringing, there is an ignorance about much doctrine and symbolism in the Church. Unless they sit down and think about it, the readers are sometimes unaware that there is a Christian background for the events and actions, and even the characters in the stories.

> ... out of about 60 reviews only two showed any knowledge that my idea of the fall of the Bent One was

---

[112] W.H. Lewis. pp. 307.

anything but an invention of my own. But if there only was someone with a richer talent and more leisure, I think that this great ignorance might be a help to the evangelization of England; any amount of theology can now be smuggled into people's minds under the cover of romance without their knowing it.[113]
(C.S. Lewis, speaking of <u>Perelandra</u>)

Some points to consider: Jesus taught with parables and fictions. Only one parable mentions God outright. The rest were just stories of familiar things. He let the symbols and ideas speak to His hearers of God. Those whose hearts were ready understood the hidden meanings. Those not ready missed it, but the seeds were planted for later understanding.

Drama was started as a religious tool, to teach the people about the gods. When the Church took over the use of drama, it found a great tool to reach the people in their hearts, and grab their imaginations. Myth and allegory, which are integral parts of the genre, were used to teach the people with fantastic, unreal stories to illustrate the way the world and the gods operated.

With so much religious character to the genre already, Christians would be fools to ignore or even oppose the use of science fiction/fantasy. It isn't necessary that the stories preach at all, or even mention God or Jesus, but they can plant the seeds of ideas and needs in the hearts of the readers, which can later bloom into a life turned over to God. Science fiction/fantasy should be claimed for God, not left to the devil's misuse.

---

[113] Ibid. pp. 167.

VIRTUES AND VICES

> Popular literature ... is the first form of mass entertainment experienced by society. Popular literature has always been criticized, been accused of having negative effects on the recipient ... Nonetheless, it fulfills quite definite functions for millions of people ... (the medium requires the reader to become engrossed in what he is reading, requires him to form his own mental image) and still constitutes a major leisure-time activity.[114]

> Even when American television has little or nothing to say, it still can say it beautifully. And when American TV does have something to say -- as with Star Trek -- the illusion is convincing enough to alter the shape of reality.[115]

One of the first arguments against fantasy, especially when produced by Christians, is about the didacticism. From the very beginning of the story, it is plain to see the fantasy world is only a thin disguise, and not very well-done at that, for a sermon. Today, much of allegory is not handled very well, making it a lost art because the treatment is neither subtle nor strong enough where needed. The writer who has a point to make must take special care not to let the idea overrun the story.

> Unfortunately, the element of didacticism is so strong, the event allegorized of such cosmic importance, the allegorical elements are out of all proportion ... the didacticism is too thinly disguised, and sometimes positively distasteful. The result is ... an uneasy and uneven mixture, and the passages of allegory float like stubborn lumps in a rather thin gruel.[116]

---

[114] Fischer and Melnik, Editors. pp. xvi.
[115] Gerrold. pp. 39.
[116] Swinfen. pp. 115.

To the other extreme are the complaints about movies or books that are only exercises in spectacle. There is nothing wrong in a section or two for fun, but the whole story should not be that way. Adventure is fine, but there should be some meaning to it. Special effects, especially if well-done, are great. But they should support the action, not appear just for the sake of flash and inflating the budget. Gratuitous special effects are just as bad and tasteless as gratuitous sex and gore.

> Obviously, a lot of modern space fantasy is merely entertainment ... a lot of it is much more than this. Science fiction's best representatives do indeed contain 'mind-expanding, heavy philosophy:' they can help us examine our mundane earthbound problems from a fresh, original viewpoint. But then it's also true -- a lot of science fiction is just 'dumb junk.'[117]

The best and most popular science fiction/fantasy stories are about people, their relationships, dreams, problems, and learning, no matter how much glitter and hardware and special effects are used. The stories that draw people back are often the ones about personalities, (some characters can't be called 'people'). The core of the story is one that might happen anywhere, in any time or place or culture, with any hardware.

> We began as a nation hostile to fantasy for three reasons. First, fantasy is fictional, and our Puritan forebears considered any deviation from sanctioned truth to be a wicked deception -- unless, of course, they believed the fictions, in which case they became witchcraft, subject to burning. Second, we embraced the Enlightenment as part of our new national identity. An inherited pastime like the fairy tale could hardly hold its own against the initial excitement of scientific and political experiments. Third, and probably most importantly, our attention as a nation is directed primarily toward material things. New scenery, new artifacts, new wealth. We have been slow to acknowledge the effect of these external things on our minds, or to investigate their relationships as symbols ...

---

[117] Short. pp. 15.

they would explain the hostility with which many readers view the entire genre, a violent antipathy which precludes recognition of the virtues or flaws of any individual work.[118]

The very reasons for violent reactions against science fiction/fantasy are clues for why there is also such a hunger for it. The world is centered on materialism and rationality. People can only believe what they can feel with their senses, and what they can manipulate. But that puts them in a quandary, because they are also spiritual creatures. Their souls and minds need feeding with things that humanism and materialism cannot provide.

The primary heretical tendency of our age is the denial of the supernatural. If it tacitly permits God to be assumed supernatural, it tries at the least to deny the intrusion of the supernatural into that tangible, manipulatable, circumscribed realm that we are accustomed to call 'natural.'[119]

Yet at the same time, fantasy helps people better understand and interact with the world. People need fantasy to stay healthy.

Fantasy is a natural human activity. It certainly does not destroy or even insult Reason; and it does not either blunt the appetite for, nor obscure the perception of, scientific veracity. On the contrary. The keener and the clearer is the reason, the better fantasy will it make. If men were ever in a state in which they did not want to know or could not perceive truth (facts or evidence) then Fantasy would languish until they were cured. If they ever get into that state (it would not seem at all impossible), Fantasy will perish, and will become Morbid Delusion.[120]

Another argument against science fiction/fantasy is that it is not real. The fact that it might once have been or someday might be real is beyond the point. Christians argue that fantasy is wrong

---

[118] Atteberry. pp. 185.
[119] Belford. Editor. pp. 12.
[120] Tolkein. pp. 54-55.

because it is not the world that God created. True. Anyone who insists that their fantasy world is the real one is in need of help.

> Good stories often introduce the marvellous or supernatural, and nothing about Story has been so often misunderstood as this. Thus, for example, Dr. Johnson ... thought that children liked stories of the marvellous because they were too ignorant to know that they were impossible. But children do not always like them, nor are those who like them always children; and to enjoy reading about fairies ... it is not necessary to believe in them. Belief is at best irrelevant; it may be a positive disadvantage. Nor are the marvels in good Story ever mere arbitrary fictions stuck on to make narrative more sensational ... The logic of a fairy tale is as strict as that of a realistic novel, though different.[121] (C.S. Lewis)

But most people know what is and is not real. They use the fantasy world for escape and refreshment. And the world is as real as the God-created one in that it has its own complex laws and holds to them.

> As the Creator creates, so man in His image is also a creator. At the same time, the writing of fantasy appears to be closely linked with man's rational being and perception of the natural world. What may at first sight seem to be a paradox lies in fact at the heart of fantasy; that is, that to create an imaginative and imaginary world it is necessary to observe faithfully the rules of logic and inner consistency which, although they may differ from those operating in our own world, must nevertheless be as true to themselves as their parallel operations are in the normal world.[122]

> ... the most successful secondary world fantasies have as their basis a religious or philosophic view of life, which may present metaphysical concepts as physical realities. Some secondary worlds are indeed so closely bound up

---

[121] Hooper. pp. 12.
[122] Swinfen. pp. 3.

with their underlying philosophies or religious purposes
that they do not attempt normal primary world realism at
all.[123]

The biggest stink raised about the genre comes from the
religious area. A superficial look may make it seem that the story
either ignores or fights religion. But in reality that is often not true.
Even when the philosophy presented is against Christian beliefs, that
doesn't mean it isn't religious. It just isn't Christian. And again, no
one has any right to expect those not of their beliefs to present books
or films concurrent with those beliefs. Any kind of belief about life
and the answers to it is religious.

>'Space fantasy,' or 'science fiction' may never even
>mention anything 'religious' in the ordinary sense of the
>word. But whenever this fiction tries to help people find
>ultimate meaning for their lives, then it is -- by definition
>-- <u>religious</u>. As a religious fiction it will often display
>very sensitive and accurate intuition of what all people
>are basically hungering and thirsting for.[124]

Science fiction/fantasy is so attractive because it reaches
beyond the known world. It forces people to grow if they have any
hope of following the path the story or idea is going down. The
reader doesn't have to agree with it, just try to understand and see
from another's viewpoint.

>Such stretching is often associated with the impulse
>toward religion, and a very good case can be made for
>calling a great deal of science fiction religious ... Religion
>in whatever form deals with the relationship of man with
>the Other, the Unknown, the <u>numinous</u>. Religious beliefs
>concern the reasons behind the universe as it is perceived
>by humans, often stress a reality beyond the human
>reality, and just as often offer a set of moral guidelines to
>be followed. SF at its most primitive as well as most
>sophisticated is constantly searching for truth, for
>patterns, for answers to what appears unanswerable. Its

---

[123] Ibid. pp. 99.
[124] Short. pp. 15.

'wonder and awe' element is akin to the wonder and awe felt by those overwhelmed by religious feelings. And codes of behavior that heroes follow in order to achieve their minor or major quests are either implicitly or explicitly realized in much SF. Science has not become God in SF. Rather, science seems to have opened many more ways towards a belief in God, in mysteries beyond mysteries, worlds beyond worlds, than would have been thought possible by skeptics, cynics, and realists of the century's earlier years. SF, in effect, is a literature with which those not willing to adhere to traditional forms of religion in secularized society are still able to ponder mysteries and explore religious questions without being sorted into a single sect or creed. SF provides a home more for the seekers than the followers, though SF writers and readers would likely resent their being called 'religious.'[125]

Science fiction/fantasy, in asking questions and presenting possibilities, helps the mind to be aware of something beyond Humanity, something they lack. It awakens and feeds the hunger for fulfillment, completion, and perfection.

... a belief in elves, fawns and fairies was better than no belief at all. It could lead to true faith. Faery lies on the borders of that lost Eden for which there is a racial ... nostalgia, hence the kinship and comradeship between men and beast and birds, even between creatures and woods, streams and trees, and the help given by birds, fish or animals to fairytale heroes in return for some kindness.[126]

And if Christians write science fiction/fantasy, the very fact of their belief will leak into the story and leave faint trails for the seeker to follow. Someone who is against the Church may come to God because of hints and ideas and hunger awakened by a genre book. "The road to fairyland is not the road to Heaven; nor even to

---

[125] Allen. Editor. pp. 8.
[126] Marion Lochhead. *Renaissance of Wonder*. (Harper & Row. San Francisco 1977) pp. 90.

Hell ... though some have held that it may lead thither indirectly by the Devil's tithe."[127]

> Fantasy can, of course, be carried to excess. It can be ill done. It can be put to evil uses. It may even delude the minds out of which it came. But of what human thing in this fallen world is that not true? Men have conceived not only of elves, but they have imagined gods, and worshiped them, even worshipped those more deformed by their author's own evil. But they have made false gods out of other materials: their notions, their banners, their monies; even the sciences and their social and economic theories have demanded human sacrifice ... Fantasy remains a human right: we make in our measure and in our derivative mode, because we are made: and not only made, but made in the image and likeness of a Maker.[128]

"There is always a danger from cultism -- as in the strange vogue of Robert Heinlein's novel *Stranger in a Strange Land* (which had a sinister effect on Charles Manson and his followers), or more recently of Erik von Daniken."[129] Neitzche started a lot of grief in the world when he preached his philosophy of supermen. When he proclaimed that God was "dead" and humans could stand alone, he created a dilemma in the soul. There was a hunger that had to be denied, because the fulfillment of that hunger had to be denied as well. But the superman idea has failed, as shown in Hitler's regime and various others, who try to run the world without God, believing Humankind is the end-all and be-all. They believe all troubles will end when the human race perfects itself. A good number of books in the genre preach that philosophy, and people eat it up. They think fulfillment will come when the human race gets into outer space and makes contact with aliens who were *just like them* long ago, but perfected themselves. "Beware of bad philosophers bearing good entertainment."[130]

2001 is a prime example of that. There was such hopelessness in the film. Though the advanced aliens are there,

---

[127] Tolkein. pp. 5.
[128] Ibid. pp. 55.
[129] Parrinder. pp. 43.
[130] Short. pp. 22.

somewhere, by the time the humans are able to get to outer space, the aliens are either gone or unreachable. It is a lonely universe. The movie hopes the human race will not be alone for long, the only living, intelligent beings in the universe, because since there is "obviously" no God, if there is no one else out there, the human race would find a strong sense of cosmic loneliness that would be more than it could live with.[131]

> So we've now reached the point where we feel we need big help in a big hurry. Therefore, instead of placing our hopes in visiting outer space in the distant future ... our here-and-now situation has become so desperate that we're now dreaming of outer space visiting us. What we now want is a 'close encounter' or 'a way' out *right now!*[132]

Yet a funny thing has happened. As people look for help from Other, it takes on characteristics of religion, and some of the characters in the stories parallel Jesus. look at the parallels in *Superman* between Superman and Christ -- an only son, sent to help, he lived as an outsider, he stood up for the downtrodden and the right way. Neitzche has the human race as supermen going *out* to change the world, but people realize how wrong they are, so they hope for supermen coming *in* to help them. Yet still, despite all the parallels, God is being denied.

> But in *Superman* we've even made another concession: we're willing to settle for the Superman of fiction. We're ready to find consolation in something totally and obviously mythological rather than letting ourselves suffer too much disappointment when something *real* from space doesn't show up. This is why we'll always 'need' Superman. Not only is the *real* not getting the job done, but it doesn't even seem to hold out much hope in that direction. As a matter of fact 'the real' has now become ominously threatening.[133]

---

[131] Ibid. pp. 23.
[132] Ibid. pp. 32.
[133] Ibid. pp. 40-42.

The need of Humankind makes it draw pictures closer to Christ because He is the ultimate fulfillment. Messiah, friend, a single man, living as a man, to show the truth and the life to the world. It is a sign of the time that imaginative books seem to be getting closer and closer to religious symbols. Not all of it, because a good deal still talks about doing right and working for the good of all, or just provides a fun adventure. But still a good number of movies show a search for a key to the meaning of life, a hunger put in people for 'something.' *Close Encounters* is a wonderful example of people who had a need and would stop at nothing, not criticism or government rules or danger to their very lives, until they had the answer. This is the way Christians should be.

> It is actually an extremely significant religious film ... that points to the deepest question and answers of all time. As such it is far more truly religious film than 99% of the overtly 'religious' schlock Hollywood has produced in the past. 'Close Encounters' is a beautiful modern-day parable, the story of a space visitation that bears uncanny resemblance to the very visitation all of us need, the visitation of Christ into our darkened hearts. No doubt these resemblances are unintended by Spielberg. But again, this only points to how many of the 'keys' manufactured by a society will, because of that society's great need, take on surprising and unexpected resemblances to the correct key -- Christ.[134]

Christians should seek in their stories to find the truth and illustrate it to others. Imaginations were given to the human race to help them understand and apply the truth of God in their lives. George MacDonald said, "It is God who gives thee thy mirror of imagination and if thou keep it clean, it will give thee back no shadow but the truth."[135] MacDonald said this "because he himself saw truth and goodness through his poetic imagination, and not dimmed by it but made more clear. In this light he saw and conveyed the Gospel. He saw into the heart of creation and into the hearts of children."[136] Can Christians do any less than seek God's

---

[134] Ibid. pp. 34.
[135] Hein. pp. x.
[136] Lochhead. pp. 20.

truth in imagination, and use it to illustrate in understandable pictures what the rest of the world is seeking?

Science fiction/fantasy is a useful and effective tool. It is bad only when it is abused.

Once an answer has been found in life, the genre can also help people understand the world around them and to understand themselves. It is strange how boldly, sometimes crudely, fantasy deals with good and evil. There *is* evil in the world, and evil people. But often parents want to shelter their children from that knowledge. That is wrong. "... reactions against fairy tales stem from our desire to have children believe that all people are good and our refusal to let children know that the source of much that goes wrong in life is due to their own nature."[137]

Of course, there is bad science fiction/fantasy, which makes evil seem more exciting, easy, and profitable than good. But these bad examples show up in all genres of literature, art, and film. That does not mean all types of fantastic fiction should be dropped. The good should be concentrated on and the bad pushed away.

> He (Plutarch) sees fiction as primarily conveying an imitative-exemplary meaning and ... bad examples are to be ignored, rejected outright, or identified as bad examples; they do not have to be construed symbolically ... so the utility of reading or teaching poetic fictions lies in applying their exemplary implications to as many analogous situations as come to mind.[138]

> The thematic structure of *The Return of the Jedi* is congruent with our belief structure, so the film has the benefit of providing an escape and, at the same time, of reinforcing many of our sacred values.[139]

It being established that science fiction/fantasy is a good way of teaching examples for living and giving answers, it should not be taken in the other extreme and treated as a textbook. Using the genre in that way will only ruin it. Science fiction/fantasy was created for

---

[137] John Aquino. *Fantasy in Literature.* pp. 17.
[138] Rollinson. pp. 6.
[139] Berger. pp. 73.

refreshing and enriching the spirit. It teaches subconsciously, by example, subliminally.

> For a fantasy to function at its best sacramentally, MacDonald felt that a person should read it simply for his own pleasure, not consciously for his edification, as he would read, say, a parable. It is, of course, intuitive perceptions that MacDonald has in mind. Mere intellectual analysis alone tends to leave the spirit emaciated, not strengthened. He is confident that to the proper reader some incidents will seem to convey moral and spiritual truths; others will remain incorrigibly enigmatic. The type and quantity of truths perceived will depend upon the reader's spiritual state and special needs at the time.[140]

Again, people find what they look for, whether consciously or unconsciously.

> The goal of fantasy is not to convince us that there are ogres or elves in another world, but to lead us through the struggles of this other world to a better understanding of our own. Fantasy bestows upon us an experience of spirit which reveals to us certain truths with which to encounter our real world. Fantasy is a sojourn in faith; an assurance of things hoped for and things not seen. But the experience of this subcreated world endows us with a vision which orders our daily life in spiritual terms. We are called to the insight of what is good in a blinding confusion between good and evil. We engage life with a clarity of perspective, a 'clearer view' which orders the demands of the age in accordance with the demands of the spirit.[141]

As to engaging attention, fantasy does so in many of the ways any fiction does: by generating suspense, by presenting characters whose fates we are interested in, by

---

[140] Hein. pp. 55.
[141] Timmerman. pp. 55-56.

appealing to our senses, by calling forth human longings and fears. However, it can, in addition, take advantage of our curiosity. When we read fantasy we explore the unknown, and that interest alone can carry an otherwise undistinguished work. A better work of fantasy can also engage us intellectually and morally by presenting the clash of ideas and issues in simple and concrete forms. More than realistic fiction, it can clarify philosophical and moral conflicts embodying them in story lines that may not be directly applicable to our own complex and muddied lives but which can please or inspire because of their open and evident design. That is one of the most important accomplishments at which fantasy can aim, to give comprehensible form to life, death, good and evil; this has always been the primary aim of the earliest kind of fantasy, the folktale.[142]

    Fantasy teaches, but it must be done well. It is a world unto itself, based in its own laws, yet at the same time, to be of any good, it must not negate basic truths and morals. This gets into a sticky situation when it comes to exploring artificial intelligence or using magical powers. The Christians especially must tread carefully. Consider this idea: the laws that would call some things evil in this world are "secondary" laws of truth. It does not apply in another world where, say, *everyone* uses magic as a matter of course. *How* the magic is used, for what purpose, is the moral issue in that world, not whether magic is permissible or not.

... a fabric of symbolism may enable the writer to create a moral and intellectual framework for the action of his novel. Symbolism allows an author to link the limited world of his characters to one of the great systems of values, so that we are made to compare the happenings in the novel with their mythological or historical parallels. Specific actions in the story illustrate general patterns of behavior, and the private character acquires a new

---

[142] Atteberry. pp. 3-4.

importance where he is seen in the light of his symbolic counterpart.[143]

This conscious and moral basis of much serious fantasy may be revealed in a number of ways. It may be implicit in the numinous quality of the marvellous experience. It may be present in the structural patterns of the work, in the use of mythic elements or in the quest tale form. Similarly, the creation of a secondary world may provide a utopia, or dystopia, or simply by its very quality of 'otherness,' cast a sharp light on a primary world. The moral basis may occur obliquely in symbolic language or in an allegorical narrative. Or it may arise in the overt discussion of moral principles.[144]

Still, taking the above into consideration, many people argue against the genre because they say it tears down values. This is not true.

The American fantasy tradition is important because fantasy is conservative. It holds ancient beliefs and insights safe within a shell of seeming inconsequence. Its roots go back beyond writing and beyond recall, but it also continues to alter as our lives change ... The fantasies that are undoubtedly being written today ... will arise from as yet unguessable troublings within American life. And they will cover those irritations -- not simply cover them over with coats of pearl but completely reshape them -- into meaningful narratives new in insight and richly traditional in form and matter.[145]

... it is not only possible but often advantageous to move one's creation way from the observable world into the realm of the impossible, where archetypal, human truths tend to lie a little closer to the surface, as in dreams.[146]

---

[143] Swinfen. pp. 100.
[144] Ibid. pp. 147.
[145] Atteberry. pp. 186.
[146] Ibid. pp. 34.

> The delight in fantasy is not in disordering, but in reordering reality. It reinforces our awareness of what is by showing us what might be, and uses the imaginary laws of the created world to postulate hidden principles on which our own might be organized.[147]

Perhaps the most important thing the genre does is help to regain the sense of wonder and freshness when the real world is examined again. After being to a far-off land, where things are so very different, it is possible to look at society as well as the physical environment with a clearer vision. "Writers are now very conscious of probing the social consequences of science and technology and of exploring the assumptions and limitations of the scientific outlook."[148] "When a literature of imaginative speculation steadfastly adheres to the conventional outlook of the community regarding heroes and standards or values, it is indeed offering the most important kind of social criticism -- unconscious social criticism."[149] Perhaps the flaws are more noticeable, but so are the beauties.

> Nevertheless -- and it is curious when one considers how individual is the world of each fantasy -- there is a very definite and constant character to fantasy, and in nothing is it perhaps so markedly constant as in its devotion to wonder at created things, and its profound sense that that wonder is above almost everything else a spiritual good not to be lost.[150]

> It is by the magical renewing and refreshment of our perceptions that we come to view the primary world, dulled through familiarity, with newly wondering eyes ... Fantasy is thus an enrichment of life, for even if dragons exist only in Otherworld, our lives in the primary world

---

[147] Ibid. pp. 36.
[148] Ibid. pp. 38.
[149] Parrinder. pp. 40.
[150] C.N. Manlove. *The Impulse of Fantasy Literature.* (Kent State University Press. Kent, Ohio 1983) pp. 156.

are richer and more beautiful simply through the imagining of them.[151]

The Christian should remind and be reminded in fantasy that this is God's world, from His hands and mind. If God has made it, then it is worth exploring with every faculty available -- not just with the senses but with the soul, spirit and mind.
To inquire into what God has made is the main function of the imagination. It is aroused by facts, is nourished by facts, seeks higher and yet higher laws in those facts: but refuses to regard science as the sole interpreter of nature, or the laws of science as the only region of discovery.[152]

Once Humanity has learned to understand the world and themselves, and then explore it better through the use of the genre, the final step is to learn how to affect the world and others, how to react and interact with it, and survive.
Fiction in which the 'other worlds' are negatively valued is not necessarily designed to make us happy docile citizens of the world today. Wells ... and others wrote with subversive intent, using a bad future to underline a bad present, and so confronting their readers with the shock of 'estrangement.' The fiction which results from such intentions falls roughly into two classes. There is the novel of extrapolation, usually set in the near future and dramatizing the threat posed by contemporary social developments; this is the continuation of literary realism by other, not very dissimilar means. More truly speculative, however, is the 'epistemological satire' which examines the limits of human nature and man's reason through the device of a parallel world, which is usually in the future but has no linear or directly historical relation to the present. Where the novel of extrapolation takes a particular problem such as overpopulation or pollution, and shows it getting disastrously worse, novels of the second kind permit a more far-reaching 'anthropological'

---

[151] Swinfen. pp. 6.
[152] Roger C. Schlobin. Editor. *The Aesthetics of Fantasy Literature and Art.* (University of Notre Dame Press. Notre Dame, Ind. 1982) pp. xiii.

examination of man himself. The novelists transcend conventional assumptions by showing us different social structures, different modes of thinking, different physiology and -- particularly in recent novels -- different kinds of sexuality.[153]

C.M. Kornbluth argues that its effectiveness as social criticism was greatly overrated; ... Robert Heinlein took the traditionalist line and praised SF as a Darwinist survival kit which was 'preparing our youngsters to be mature citizens of the galaxy.'[154]

... fantasy, just as much as the 'realist' novel, is about reality -- about the human condition. All serious fantasy is deeply rooted in human experience and is relevant to human living. Its major difference from the realist novel is that it takes account of areas of experience -- imaginative, subconscious, visionary -- which free the human spirit to range beyond the limits of empirical primary world reality. In a sense, then, fantasy provides the writer with greater scope to construct his own scheme of morality, his own time stricture, his own political and social order. But at no time does this apparent freedom permit the author to escape from contemporary reality. Indeed the fundamental purpose of serious fantasy is to comment upon the real world and to explore moral, philosophical and other dilemmas posed by it. This process may be described less as didacticism, although this is sometimes present, than as a form of creative questioning; and it may be argued, without such questioning in any intellectual field, there can be no advance.[155]

Again, people must take care what fantasies they read, write, and watch, because sometimes the subconscious effect is greater than the conscious effect they are aware of. "A fantasy is a journey.

---

[153] Parrinder. pp. 47.
[154] Ibid. pp. 39.
[155] Swinfen. pp. 231.

It is a journey into the subconscious mind, just as psychoanalysis is. Like psychoanalysis it can be dangerous; *and it will change you.*"[156] A child who grows up with heroes surely has a better idea of what good people should be like and how they act, by example, than a child who has only had rules and platitudes preached at him. It is easier to get a child to behave and think rightly by having an attractive, strong, and wise role model, than it is just by telling him how he should behave and believe. The child will start out emulating the role model before ever thinking about right and wrong, so role models must be chosen carefully.

> The destiny of the world is determined less by the battles that are lost and won than by the stories it loves and believes in.[157]

The heroes presented to today's youth and adults should be ones who win first because they are good, and then because they are wise and talented, not just because they're as strong and cunning as evil. Maybe that's where the Church is also falling down. It isn't presenting heroes, or presenting them properly, to the children.

For the Christian, science fiction/fantasy should be used to augment the teachings of the Church, not replace them. By examples and stories that are new, the stories should show how to live and how to respond to the world and its problems. "The fantasist responds to destructiveness by building, to disorder by imagining order, and to despair by calling forth wonder."[158]

> The hope, the anticipation of fantasy and mythic literature is that by bringing a power larger than man but apparent through man to bear upon this world, we can once again kindle the light of the human spirit. The nature of that power ... is constituted of enduring and indomitable values such as heroism, chivalry, a sense of good over against evil.[159]

To see the truth in Fantasy we need Recovery: a recovery of sight and insight, of a healthy imagination; a recovery

---

[156] Timmerman. pp. 3.

[157] Luke. pp. 1.

[158] Atteberry. pp. 186.

[159] Timmerman. pp. 28.

which can come only from humility ... We should meet fairy-tale centaurs and dragons and then discover, really discover, dogs and sheep and horses. This was Chesterton's assertion too. Fairy-tales can be wholesome medicine, healing herbs, purifying mind and imagination (as *Phantastes* did for C.S. Lewis). They can bring renewal, soundness of mental health, wholeness and wholesomeness which comes closest to holiness.[160]

---

[160] Lochhead. pp. 104.

THE PSYCHOLOGY OF SCIENCE FICTION/FANTASY

> Everyone ... who feels the story will read its meaning after his own nature and development ... Your meaning may be superior to mine.[161] (George MacDonald)

The effect of any book or film depends on the maturity or immaturity of the reader/viewer. It doesn't matter what the genre -- there are always those emotionally/mentally/ spiritually immature enough to fall into the trap of the world presented to them, and take that as reality. When I was in college, I was home one afternoon to catch a local afternoon talk show (Please don't ask me what channel, let alone the name of the show. It's too long ago! I just remember the incident, not the people.) The guests for the day were an actor and actress for a popular soap opera. After they left, a woman called up and berated the hostess for having such "morally low" people on the show (the man played a pimp and the woman a prostitute). The caller had been so drawn into the false world of the soap opera, she thought the people actually were the characters they played. The hostess realized this and tried to explain it to the woman, whose response was to scream at the hostess and tell her that *she* didn't know what was real.

This sort of thing happens in all genres. But, because it seems more obvious when people fall into a fantasy world, that is what gets most of the attention.

There are perils when fantasy loses its link to reason and fact. Some people we call mentally ill are simply more at home in the precinct of fantasy. There are other people, however, and we call them 'sane,' who tremble to approach its borders, afraid perhaps that they will never get back. They are the dull, predictable drudges of the world, living starved and shrunken lives. If they ever do have a vision they are terrified by it, scared that if they

---

[161] Hein. pp. xix.

admitted it they might land with the so-called 'mentally ill' inside asylum bars.[162]

This brings up a problem of the times. People have been trained to think of their own see-able, touchable corner of the world as the only reality, that anything beyond their experience is beyond their imagining, probably because they have lost a good deal of the ability to imagine. This is dangerous. People lose their ability to balance humility as well as pride. They are lost and alone.

Man ... has been trained to concentrate on such a limited portion of reality that he has been brainwashed almost as successfully as if he lived under a Communist or Fascist regime. He has forgotten the depths and complexity of his own psyche (or soul or personality, call it what you will), and the kind of knowledge that can touch it. He believes that everything he knows comes to him consciously, as a product of his reason and his senses, which tell him that he is one tiny outgrowth of an obviously physical universe. Man finds himself a speck on a limitless plain of energy and matter, none of which speaks with any certainty about God or any other religious reality. The fact that this idea of the world seems so obvious, however, should alert us to ask some questions. It is very often the obvious things, those we accept at face value without reading the fine print, that need to be examined the most carefully.[163]

Our loss of the capacity for festivity and fantasy also has profound religious significance. The religious man is one who grasps his own life within a larger historical and cosmic setting ... But without real festive occasions and without the nurture of fantasy man's spirit as well as his psyche shrinks. He becomes something less than a man, a gnat with neither origin nor destiny.[164]

---

[162] Harvey Cox. *The Feast of Fools*. (Harper & Row. NY 1969) pp. 62.
[163] Kelsey. pp. 2.
[164] Cox. pp. 14.

What these psychologists found is that the sense of loss of meaning could result in a host of psychological and physical illnesses. Although not all psychological illness has this root, the loss of direction and purpose is often a common cause of such illness in the modern world.[165]

Imagination can be harmful if it takes over one's life. That is the opposite extreme of the damage that can be done from allowing no imagination or imaginative life at all. Imagination is given to humans to help them, to work for the future, keep them from harm, finding ways to fill needs and even work off anger and questions by picturing what could happen without really doing the imagined action. It is a type of safety valve or fuse.

... psychological harm can be done when the unconscious is repressed; however, when unconscious material is permitted to come to awareness and is worked through in imagination, its harmful potential is reduced, and some of its force can be made to serve positive purposes.[166]

The survival of mankind as a species has also been placed in jeopardy by the repression of festivity and fantasy. This is because man inhabits a world of constant change, and in such a world both festival and fantasy are indispensable for survival. If he is to survive man must be both innovative and adaptive.[167]

Imagination helps people understand their problems by helping to picture them in a new way.

The fairy-tale is therapeutic because the patient finds his *own* solutions, through contemplation of what the story seems to imply about him and his inner conflicts at this moment in his life. The content of the chosen tale usually has nothing to do with the patient's external life, but much to do with his inner problems, which seem incomprehensible and hence unsolvable. The fairy-tale

---

[165] Kelsey. pp. 91.
[166] John Aquino. *Fantasy in Literature*. pp. 10.
[167] Cox. pp. 12.

clearly does not refer to the outer world, although it may begin realistically enough and have everyday features woven into it. The unrealistic nature of these tales (which narrow-minded rationalists object to) is an important device, because it makes obvious that the fairy-tale's concern is not useful information about the external world, but inner processes taking place in an individual.[168]

Fantasy and imagination are necessary for the proper emotional and psychological development in children. Without it, they have a warped, one-sided view of the world, or they don't know what to expect or have any way to react to survive. Without fantasy and story, they have no real example set before them in their short lives, and no experience to go by.

Like the classic fairy-tale, *The Return of the Jedi* has a 'happy ending.' This is necessary to give the young child, who is using the fairy-tale to learn about life to gain courage, a sense that he or she has possibilities, can triumph even though the odds ... seem hopeless. Thus, Luke ultimately 'redeems' his father, via the power of love, by forcing his father to triumph over the spirit of evil that has dominated him.[169]

Children have to be taught to want to learn. "Fantasy literature, based on the premise of 'what if' introduces the child to the wonders of inquiry."[170] Imagination, as well as being a healthy way to learn and work as a safety valve, also makes children more manageable and able to handle themselves in new situations.

... children who have vivid and fanciful imaginations can sit quietly longer than less imaginative youngsters, are less aggressive, and tell more creative stories ... fantasy/play is a precursor of adult competence, providing the basis for useful problem solving and for language development ... if the fantasy life is not

---

[168] Bruno Bettelheim. *The Uses of Enchantment.* (Alfred A. Knopf. NY 1977) pp. 25.
[169] Berger. pp. 72.
[170] Aquino. pp. 18.

developed by adulthood, the individual tends to be less relaxed, less independent, and more bored than imaginative people.[171]

The imagination is the bridge between fantasy and reality, the spiritual and physical sides of life. it makes people healthy and strong, and teaches them. Imagination, fantasy, myth, drama, etc., are links to God. This has been called a rainbow bridge inside people. The rainbow, in many mythologies, linked heaven and earth. In Genesis, a rainbow was a sign of promise and hope.

The rainbow signifies the divine presence, hope, reconciliation and rebirth. It often appears after a storm ... a symbol of hope and promise. The imagination is our inner rainbow in many ways. It is the bridge which joins God and the earth, the sacred and the secular, bringing them into unity in our life. The imagination enables us to live in multi-levelled, multi-colored truth, and to receive the truth which is pervaded by mist and mystery. It is also the human power that opens us to possibility and promise, the not-yet of the future. In all these ways, the imagination is essential to Christian faith.[172]

---

[171] Ibid. pp. 11.
[172] Kathleen R. Fischer. *The Inner Rainbow*. (Paulist Press. NY 1983) pp. 7.

CHRISTIAN FICTION AND ENTERTAINMENT

> But if believers don't write ... those who don't understand the Christian message will. Too often, secular film writers and other strictly profit-oriented film professionals do not present the Christian message as spiritual minded viewers expect it should be. To many believers, secular films about the Bible or other spiritual subjects often are not faithful to the original concepts as Christians understand them.[173]

A great majority of the films made today with any kind of religious feel to them are not made by Christians. The filmmakers are either searching for a meaning in life, or think they have found it and want to share it. Because of the religious parallels or themes that seem Christian, a great many Christians think the film and its maker have to be Christian as well, and there is an uproar when the rest of the movie doesn't pan out as purely Christian. Think of the trouble with Star Wars and the Force.

Christians have no right to demand that an artist's visions stay true to the Gospel because he borrowed a few ideas from the Bible and liturgy. What needs to be done is for Christians to get involved in making films in all genres and have the true Christian message in them.

> Since the major matter of religious tradition are conveyed in recognizable literary forms, especially narrative, the dependence of religion on literature and the study of religion on literary criticism cannot go unrecognized indefinitely.[174]

A film that preaches is a talking head, not a dramatic production. The problem is, many Christians think that any kind of Christian movie, book, etc., has to be blatantly, identifiably

---

[173] William Gentz. Editor. *Writing to Inspire*. (Writers Digest Books. Cincinnati 1982) pp. 7.
[174] Wesley A. Hart. *Moral Fiber*. (Fortress Press. Philadelphia 1982) pp. 1.

Christian, and that is reducing it to the level of propaganda. It runs and ruins the story, unless it happens to be allegorical in form and content to begin with.

As a writer in the field of religion you may be inclined to begin with 'theme' as you look for a story idea. There is nothing wrong with this, except that you might wind up with more of a sermon than a story, and no editor wants this. Editors even of the Sunday school weeklies beg us not to send them 'moralizing' stories. The moral will be there, but leave it implied. Show your reader in story action, instead of telling him or her outright, that love and faithfulness are great virtues. Pay most attention to strong character development, so far as there is room for it.[175]

Lewis once said to a group of friends that he had never started a story with the idea of a moral or message. 'The story itself should force its moral upon you. You find out what the moral is by writing the story.'[176]

Fiction is a story, not a sermon. Any reader with the sensitivity to get the message in a story is going to know when he is preached at, and he will stop right there and never read it again, and likely tell others not to waste their time with it. In the theater, it is said that if a message is to be sent, use Western Union. The same is true for writing fiction of any kind. If there is a message, an idea that the writer wants to get across, it should be shown by innuendo and example, hinted at. The readers should be made curious, so they will think and discover the truth for themselves. The idea will stick with them longer if they think it through for themselves instead of being told flat out what to think, what to believe, etc. "For fiction, of all the forms of literature, presents the broadest judgment of life; in the phrase of a brilliant Frenchman, it is the 'metaphor of a philosophy.'"[177]

---

[175] John A. Moore. *Write for the Religion Market*. (Etc. Publishers. Palm Springs 1981) pp. 86.
[176] Belford. Editor. pp. 32.
[177] Henry Bett. MA. *Studies in Literature*. (The Epworth Press. London 1929) pp. 9.

Unfortunately, Christian literature was once so rare that editors were willing to take almost anything they could get. Christian literature was a mass of badly disguised preaching. Once in a while a gem would be found in the trash, and shone even brighter because of the poor quality of the rest of what was offered.

> The need of Christian writing has always been great and there was a day when less skilled writers were nurtured along by dedicated religious press editors. That day is long gone! Competition is keen. The best of writing is needed in the inspirational field and the rest of inspirational writing will cross over into other fields.[178]

The reader should be teased with hints of hidden meaning. How better to get a reader interested in the rest of more blatant fiction than to hook him with subtle works, with good style and exciting stories? Christians are made in the image of God, and He created a lavish, lush, colorful world. Why shouldn't the work of Christians be the same way? They can talk about life from the Christian perspective and still be interesting to non-Christians. These writers must be creative and skilled. Just because the writing is Christian is no excuse for it being poor in terms of character, setting, story, and events.

> Storytelling as a rhetorical art is one of the most ancient and effective tools of communication among human societies. For centuries this impressive instrument of thought and expression has served both as a means of getting together as well as a source of amusement among human groups. At the same time it has played a significant role in promoting spiritual harmony and social consensus within groups.[179]

> ... success in sacred literature depends on the same qualities of structure, suspense, variety, diction and the like which secure success in secular literature.[180]

---

[178] Gentz. pp. i.
[179] Fischer and Melnik. Editors. pp. 43.
[180] C.S. Lewis. *Christian Reflections*. pp. 23.

> Artists are makers of form. They share in their own way
> an incarnation, the embodiment of spirit in matter.
> Christian spirituality needs the arts because such
> symbolic expression is vital to personal growth.[181]

Story affects people whether they are aware of it or not. A well-made story will stick in the consciousness longer because it was enjoyable, the mental pictures were clearer, richer, the characters and events more real. The ideas will work in the subconscious, combining with other ideas, and become part of the reader's ideology or personality.

> But to enrich his life, it must stimulate his imagination;
> help him to develop his intellect and to clarify his
> emotions; be attuned to his anxieties and aspirations; give
> full recognition to his difficulties while at the same time
> suggesting solutions to the problem which perturbs him.
> In short, it must at one and the same time relate to all
> aspects of his personality -- and this without ever
> belittling but on the contrary, giving full credence to the
> seriousness of the child's predicaments, while
> simultaneously promoting confidence in himself and in
> his future.[182]

> What comes out ... should have the ring of truth in the
> little world you have created for your reader during the
> (time) he spends with your story. You can even hope that
> his life will be influenced for good, even if it is a
> lighthearted story resulting only in the warmth of a
> smile.[183]

Just what is wrong with entertainment and good feelings from a story? Science fiction/fantasy has been called escapist literature, in scorn. But really, isn't escape necessary in the foul mess of the world today? The really good literature and films of all time, though, are the ones which help the reader-viewers escape, and then come back changed, even if only in little ways. Maybe the people

---

[181] Fischer. pp. 57.
[182] Bettelheim. pp. 5.
[183] Moore. pp. 88.

learned how to handle problems. Maybe they gained courage or optimism because they saw others who were worse off, who still triumphed. "Remember that symbol is a way of expressing truth -- it does not denote something that is not true."[184] A lot can be learned, therefore, even from "feel-good" movies.

This puts even more responsibility on writers and filmmakers. They must build more concrete and believable worlds. They must make laws for the world to stand on, and these laws must never be broken during the story. Even if the world is totally impossible, as long as it stays true to the inner laws of its own, the reader will be able to believe in it and not find fault.

> What really happens is that the story-maker proves a successful 'sub-creator.' He makes a Secondary World which your mind can enter. Inside it, what he relates is 'true': it accords with the laws of the world. You therefore believe it, while you are, as it were, inside. The moment disbelief arises, the spell is broken; the magic, or rather, art, has failed.[185]

The story must be real to the participant for any effect to be accomplished. Christian writers and filmmakers must especially keep this in mind. Since they deal with the ultimate truth of all, Jesus Christ, it is somehow easier to fall into the trap of preaching and unreality. Any teaching in the story must be natural, a part of the story. The events must not become secondary to the sermon someone preaches within it. Christians have a great duty to perform and must not fail.

> So writing becomes our ministry. We are commissioned not just to write evil down, but to write God up. We are instructed to teach, to train, to interpret, to inform, to edify, to kindle the imagination, to narrate stories as Jesus did, and even to entertain. We are to provide milk for children, solid food for full-grown men and women, and the elixir of poetry to express our love for our Creator. We are to write about good and evil, frustration and victory, justice and mercy, sin and redemption, joy and

---

[184] Belford. pp. 14.
[185] Tolkein. pp. 37.

adversity, and always grace and glory. We are to cover the waterfront of human experience, to run the gamut of life, and so give people a handle to grasp as they seek to attain a worthwhile and productive existence under Christ.[186]

Story establishes world in myth, defends such established world in apologue, discusses and describes world in action, attacks world in satire, and subverts world in parable.[187]

---

[186] Gentz. pp. 18.
[187] John Dominic Crossan. *The Dark Interval*. (Argus Communications. Allen, Texas 1975) pp. 9.

FILM

> The film and its power were predicted in the Bible. There's to be a universal language making all men understand each other. We are taking the first baby steps in a power that could bring about the millennium. Remember that when you stand in front of the camera.[188]
> (D.W. Griffith)

Film speaks to all people, regardless of language or upbringing. In the early days of film, when it was silent, it sometimes taught immigrants, who could not speak English, about America. Naturally, those with vision could see the effect that film would have. Very early on, people were asking, "Is there any reason why so compelling a force cannot be thrown entirely to the aid of education and inspiration?"[189] Police records told of people copying the crimes depicted in films they saw. "It is probably the greatest single force in shaping the American character."[190]

> The function of art is to enable. Art is as much a servant and tool of civilization as science. Its utility, especially to youth, is as vicarious experience, food for imaginative stimulus -- and who will argue for the education of youth by evil adventure and stimulus, no matter how real in fact or realistic in artistic representation?[191]

Imagination is often thought a property of the young or the artistic. Hence, a medium that appeals to the imagination and gives experiences is a mighty force. People could see the potential good and bad influences on the forming minds of the youth, and they were understandably concerned. Those who saw motion pictures as good pressed the argument against those who fought film, saying it all was bad. As one supporter of film said:

---

[188] Kevin Brownlow. "Lilian Gish." *American Film.* (April, 1984) pp. 22.
[189] Gerald Mast. Editor. *The Movies in Our Midst.* (University of Chicago Press. Chicago 1982) pp. 60.
[190] Ibid. pp. 61.
[191] Ibid. pp. 340.

> ... its higher purposes consist of the presentation and encouragement of the right ideals and right conduct in life and living ... God and evil may be contrasted; wrong motives as well as right motives may be presented, and there is no need of tiresome insistence that virtue is its own reward. But good and evil must not be confused; good must be presented as good and evil as evil.[192]

Already they were setting standards for what should be presented. Those who were aware of the growing popularity and force of the film knew of its effect already.

> When an enterprise as vast as this gets into the field of morals, something serious is bound to happen one way or another ... With young, formative and impressionable minds the results are of course, worse. Indeed, the motion picture show is as widely suggestive to this class as the deep sensational novel used to be.[193]

The men who made the films know that they had to be publicly involved in the concern over the morals and effects of their works. Some only did it to protect their control over film and the profits that were sure to mount up. So boards of censorship were set up around the country, starting in New York, at the request of motion-picture exhibitors. This was used to stay on the good side of concerned citizens, as well as shut out pictures they did not approve of.[194]

Later, it was found that movies not only influenced the development of morals in the young, but could bring about changes in public attitude. Film was used during war efforts to support patriotism.[195] And today, for anyone who knows what to look for, attempts in film to influence the public attitudes towards political topics, patriotism, and other social issues, are very clear. Why shouldn't Christians use film as well? After all, the Church has the most important message of all to convey.

---

[192] Ibid. pp. 341.
[193] Ibid. pp. 59.
[194] Ibid. pp. 144.
[195] Ibid. pp. 163

> The Fantastic or Mythical is a mode available to all ages for some readers ... At all ages, if it is well used by author and meets the right reader, it has the same power: to generalize while remaining concrete, to present in palpable form not concepts or even experiences, but whole classes of experience, and to throw off irrelevancies. But at its best it can do more: it can give us experience we have never had and thus, instead of commenting on life, can add to it.[196]

Science fiction/fantasy can teach and form just as effectively as the motion picture. Often in fairytales, the main use was to teach and record tradition and truth. It is for every age and every member of the family. It isn't just for children, though they do benefit more from it, being so open while their elders have learned to close their minds to any subtle teaching that might be in the narrative. As C.S. Lewis said:

> It is usual to speak in a playfully apologetic tone about one's adult enjoyment of what are called 'children's' books. I think the convention a silly one. No book is really worth reading at the age of ten which is not equally ... worth reading at the age of fifty ... The only imaginative works we ought to grow out of are those which it would have been better not to have read at all.[197]

Whoever started the saying that what is good for you won't taste good or be any fun, was wrong. The Proverbs state innumerable times that wisdom and truth were greater treasures than anything materialistic that anyone could hope for. Truth and learning can be wrapped comfortably in beautiful words.

As well as relegating fantasy to the playroom, imagination as a whole is looked down on. Some people will have nothing to do with speculative fiction, (yet find nothing wrong with soap operas or dime westerns) because they say it unfits people for the harsh realities of life in the real world. They seem to emphasize the word *real* as if it were a charm to make them wiser, stronger, and thus

---

[196] C.S. Lewis. *Of Other Worlds*. (Harcourt Brace Jovanovich. NY 1966) pp. 38.
[197] Ibid. pp. 15.

better suited to handle their trouble. But God is a God of creativity, beauty and extravagance. Look at the glorious world He made. Why can't His creatures be creative, use their imaginations to create more beauty, other worlds in their imaginations, and then learn about life within their confines? A book on another planet deals just as realistically with life, or it just isn't workable. If something clicks false, the readers can't enjoy the book no matter how hard they try to believe it. All works of fiction must have real rules, grounded in fact, to build the story on. In this new environment, the reader learns about good and bad people, interacting with each other, learning, growing, with emotions and needs just like real people. A book delving into the fantastic is not dangerous.

> It might be expected that such a book would unfit us for the harshness of reality and send us back to our daily lives unsettled and discontented. I do not find that it does so ... the whole story, paradoxically enough, strengthens our relish for real life. This excursion into the preposterous sends us back with renewed pleasure to the actual.[198] (C.S. Lewis)

If people can learn about reality through fantasy, couldn't they learn about the ultimate reality, God, through fantasy as well? For many, the fantasy story may be the only way to reach them with the Gospel because they refuse to read a Bible or study book, or sit down in a church pew, or listen to a radio preacher. Some people run at the mention of religion. But clothe it in fantasy, and they will swallow it like a sugar-coated pill and never know it is good for them until it starts to work in their subconscious, begins to affect their thinking and opinions, and makes them want something for their souls. In *Out of the Silent Planet*, C.S. Lewis pretends he is writing a true adventure of a friend as a fiction, because he and the man "agreed that the true story would not be believed by the reading public, and that it should, therefore, be presented as fiction."[199] That's what Jesus did with the Parables. He hid the truth inside little stories. Those who were mature enough to understand did so.

---

[198] Ibid. pp. 14-15.
[199] Evan K. Gibson. *C.S. Lewis: Spinner of Tales*. (Christian University Press. Washington, D.C. 1980) pp. 27.

Lewis himself preferred fantasy as a medium to share the Gospel because of a strict religious upbringing and feelings of resentment and guilt he grew up with. He felt dragons guarded the gates of the church and always watched him when he entered in, taking all the enjoyment out of the worship experience.

> Why did one find it so hard to feel as one was told one ought to feel about God or about the sufferings of Christ? I thought the chief reason was that one was told one ought to. An obligation to feel can freeze feelings. And reverence itself did harm. The whole subject was associated with lowered voices; almost as if it were something medical. But supposing that by casting all these things into our imaginary world, stripping them of our stained-glass and Sunday school associations, one could make them for the first time appear in their real potency? Could one not thus steal past those watchful dragons?[200]

Fantasy offers itself, instead of forcing itself down people's throats. The film or fiction book is made for entertainment. No one buys a book or goes to the theater under duress or to be preached at. Hence, if the Gospel is clothed in something that outwardly is only to entertain, the reader or viewer is more receptive to what might be said in the story. Each one is relaxed and more open to liking the characters and wanting to understand what makes them tick. Let just one seed be planted, and there is a chance to reach that soul completely with the Gospel.

Christians must use the film industry and take it over as they are slowly taking back the drama for the use of the Church. Drama started out as worship form, and it can be one again. Why can't film be used to worship and adore God? Movies must spread theology in a way the masses can understand.

> Movies are for the masses what theology is for an elite ... for nowhere is the distance between technics and thought so pronounced as between those who provide ... fables which feed the dreams of the world and those engaged in ... faith in search of understanding. Postmodern man

---

[200] Lewis. pp. 37.

seeks greater understanding. If he is abandoning faith, it is often because the traditional mode of representing religion does not aid understanding in our 'jet-nuclear-space' age. Thus faith no longer seems relevant to many people, even to those raised within a religious subculture.[201]

There are those who think film is sinful, and only lost souls can enjoy it. To even suggest putting a film in church, or that a film could have Christian content would give them all heart attacks at the very least. But film has been shown to be important for regular education. It can be even more valuable for religious education. Children who will not sit still for a Sunday school lesson, complete with records and flannel boards, will sit entranced watching a movie screen. And when questioned about it afterwards, they remember more from the movie than the other method. Motion pictures capture young minds with motion, sound, color, and excitement.

Unfortunately, educators, parents and cultural guardians of society have been late to recognize their potential to form and inform, thus creating the bases of communicating through shared experiences at the affective and cognitive levels.[202]

... both motion picture and theology work with transcendence, with the difference that the latter is an elite enterprise and the former oriented to the masses. While seeking recreation, diversion and understanding, movie watchers are often exercising transcendental faculties of insight, criticism, and wonder that come remarkably close to what religion has termed faith, prophesy, and reverence. A wedding of the two is overdue ...[203]

If people are already experiencing these feelings, why not give them something to think about and remember, with spiritual meat? Why not plant the seed of the Gospel that will be associated

---

[201] Neil P. Hurley. *Theology Through Film*. (Harper & Row. NY 1970) pp. ix.
[202] Ibid. pp. 5.
[203] Ibid. pp. x.

with a feeling of reverence, awe, or joy? The feelings will help an idea grow. Christianity is not just intellectual. It is emotional, too. Worship is not just preaching, but singing. Why can't the film be used, since it is already so available?

Since science fiction/fantasy films are so popular, what better place to start bringing in the Gospel?

IMPLICATIONS/CONCLUSIONS

> It might be expected that such a book would unfit us for the harshness of reality and send us back to our daily lives unsettled and discontented ... the whole story, paradoxically enough, strengthens our relish for real life. This excursion into the preposterous sends us back with renewed pleasure for the actual.[204]
>
> (C.S. Lewis)

Of course there is potential for danger in science fiction/fantasy. Anything that has the power to affect and change people's lives and thoughts can be a danger. In the same way, the *Gospel* is dangerous. When *people* are involved, there is always danger. People warp what could be beneficial into something harmful. Look what the Inquisition did with the Bible.

Admittedly, much science fiction/fantasy denies God as the Bible defines Him. The authors try to make definitions of God, truth, and goodness to fit their own desires for freedom. God can't be "rewritten," but they try anyway because the Bible is nonsense to them. Remember, God's ways are not Man's ways. Many authors are totally against recognizable religion because of the pain, the fakers and the disillusionment they have encountered, but they don't realize this was all caused by people who were making their own rules about the God they profess to serve. The problems come when people do as they please, not when people love and serve God in spirit and in truth.

Christians don't dare ignore anything as permeating and powerful as science fiction/fantasy. Any tool that is put down by Christians will be picked up by Satan. Is this the tool's fault? If people use hammers to bash in each other's heads instead of building houses, should all hammers be destroyed? No. The hammers should be taken away from the ones who misuse them and given to people who know and can facilitate the proper use of them. Christians must learn the *constructive* use of the tool of science fiction/fantasy,

---

[204] Hooper. pp. 14.

instead of concentrating on the *destructive* use, and condemning the tool because of it.

When a sermon will not reach the audience, and a fitting non-fiction story can't be found for the need, fiction will carry the theme with no trouble at all. Sometimes the idea needed to be gotten across to the audience can be carried no other way than in a science fiction/fantasy story where it is fitted into ...

> ... the symbols of things and acts, in what is commonly (not very satisfactorily) called fantasy. A common thread among their diverse purposes is keeping us conscious of the supernatural, which means keeping us conscious of the omnipotence and omnipresence of God possibly more effectively than any other medium of story can do.[205] (Edmund Fuller)

---

[205] Belford. Editor. pp. 13.

SOURCES

Allen, Dick. Editor. *Science Fiction. The Future.* 2nd Edition. Harcourt Brace Jovanovich, Inc. NY, 1983.

Aquino, John. *Fantasy in Literature.* National Education Association. Washington, D.C. 1977.

Aquino, John. *Science Fiction as Literature.* National Education Association. Washington, D.C.1976.

Atteberry, Brian. *The Fantasy Tradition in American Literature.* Indiana University Press, Bloomington, Ind. 1980.

St. Augustine. *On Christian Doctrine.* Great Books of the Western World, Vol. 18. Robert Maynard Hutchins, Editor in Chief. Encyclopedia Brittanica, Inc. Chicago, 1952.

Belford, Lee A. Editor. *Religious Dimensions in Literature.* Seabury Press. NY, 1982.

Berger, Arthur Asa. "The Return of the Jedi: The Rewards of Myth." *Society.* Vol. 21, #4. May/June, 1984.

Bett. Henry. *Studies in Literature.* The Epworth Press. London, 1929.

Bettelheim, Bruno. *The Uses of Enchantment.* Alfred A. Knopf. NY, 1977.

Bloomfield, Morton W. Editor. *Allegory, Myth and Symbol.* Harvard University Press. Cambridge, Mass. 1981.

Breen, Myles and Corcoran, Farrel. "Myth in the Television Discourse." *Communication Monographs.* Vol. 49, #2. June, 1982.

Brownlow, Kevin. "Lilian Gish." *American Film*. 1984.

Campbell, Joseph. *The Hero with a Thousand Faces*. Princeton University Press. Princeton, NJ, 1949.

Carter, Paul A. *The Creation of Tomorrow*. Columbia University Press. NY, 1977.

Cox, Harvey. *The Feast of Fools*. Harper & Row. NY, 1969.

Crossan, John Dominic. *The Dark Interval*. Argus Communications. Allen, Texas, 1975.

Cunningham, Adrian. Editor. *The Theory of Myth*. Sheed and Ward. London, 1973.

Fischer, Heinz-Deitrich, PhD., and Melnik, Stefan Reinhard, MA. Editors. *Entertainment: A Cross-Cultural Examination*. Hastings House Publishers. NY, 1979.

Fischer, Kathleen R. *The Inner Rainbow*. Paulist Press. NY, 1983.

Gentz, William. Editor. *Writing to Inspire*. Writers Digest Books. Cincinnati, 1982.

Gerrold, David. *The World of Star Trek*. BlueJay Books, Inc. NY, 1984.

Gibson, Evan K. *C.S. Lewis: Spinner of Tales*. Christian University Press. Washington, D.C. 1980.

Gould, Eric. *Mythical Intentions in Modern Literature*. Princeton University Press. Washington, D.C. 1980.

Hart, Dabney Adams. *Through the Open Door*. University of Alabama Press. Birmingham, 1984.

Hart, Wesley A. *Moral Fiber*. Fortress Press. Philadelphia, 1982.

Sources

Hein, Rollan. *The Harmony Within*. Christian University Press. Grand Rapids, 1982.

Hooper, Walter. Editor. *C.S. Lewis on Stories and Other Essays*. Harcourt Brace Jovanovich, Publishers. NY, 1982.

Hurley, Neil P. *Theology Through Film*. Harper & Row. NY, 1982.

Kelsey, Morton T. *Myth, History and Faith*. Paulist Press. NY, 1974.

Lewis, C.S. *Christian Reflections*. Wm. B. Eerdmans Publishing Company. Grand Rapids, 1967.
...*Of Other Worlds*. Harcourt Brace Jovanovich. NY, 1966.
...*On Stories*. 1982.

Lewis, W.H. Editor. *Letters of C.S. Lewis*. Harcourt Brace Jovanovich, Publishers. NY, 1966.

Lochhead, Marion. *Renaissance of Wonder*. Harper & Row. San Francisco, 1977.

Lowry, Shirly Park. *Familiar Mysteries*. Oxford University Press. Oxford, 1982.

Luke, Helen M. *The Inner Story*. Crossroad Publishing Co. NY, 1982.

Manlove, C.N. *The Impulse of Fantasy Literature*. Kent State University Press. Kent, Ohio, 1983.

Mast, Gerald. Editor. *The Movies in Our Midst*. University of Chicago Press. Chicago, 1982.

Molesworth, Charles. "Some Paragraphs on Close Encounters." *Journal of American Culture*. Vol. 2, #2. 1979.

Moore, John A. *Write for the Religion Market*. Etc. Publishers. Palm Springs, Ca. 1981.

Parrinder, Patrick. "The Black Wave: Science and Social Consciousness in Modern Science Fiction." *Radical Science Journal.* #5. 1977.

Phillips, Michael. Editor. *Philosophy and Science Fiction.* Prometheus Books. Buffalo, NY, 1984.

Rollinson, Phillip. *Classical Theories of Allegory and Christian Culture.* Duquesne University Press. Pittsburgh, 1981.

Ruthven, K.K. *Myth.* Methuen and Co., Ltd. London, 1976.

Schlobin, Roger C. Editor. *The Aesthetics of Fantasy Literature and Art.* University of Notre Dame Press. Notre Dame, Ind. 1982.

Short, Robert. *The Gospel from Outer Space.* Harper & Row. San Francisco. 1983.

Slusser, George E. and Rabbin, Eric S. and Scholes, Robert. Editors. *Bridges to Fantasy.* Southern Illinois University Press. Carbondale. 1982.

Slusser, George E. and Guffey, George R. and Rose, Mark. Editors. *Bridges to Science Fiction.* Southern Illinois University Press. Carbondale. 1980.

Swinfen, Ann. *In Defense of Fantasy.* Routledge & Kegan Paul. Boston. 1984.

Timmerman, John M. *Other Worlds: The Fantasy Genre.* Bowling Green University Popular Press. Bowling Green, Ohio. 1983.

Tolkein, J.R.R. *Tree and Leaf.* Houghton Mifflin Co. Boston, 1964.

Tyrell, Wm. Blake. "Star Trek's Myth of Science." *Journal of American Culture.* Vol. 2, #2. 1979.

About the Author

On the road to publication, Michelle fell into fandom in college and has 40+ stories in various SF and fantasy universes. She has a bunch of useless degrees in theater, English, film/communication, and writing. Even worse, she has over 100 books and novellas with multiple small presses, in science fiction and fantasy, YA, suspense, women's fiction, and sub-genres of romance.

Her official launch into publishing came with winning first place in the Writers of the Future contest in 1990. She was a finalist in the EPIC Awards competition multiple times, winning with *Lorien* in 2006 and *The Meruk Episodes, I-V,* in 2010, and was a finalist in the Realm Award competition, in conjunction with the Realm Makers convention.

Her training includes the Institute for Children's Literature; proofreading at an advertising agency; and working at a community newspaper. She is a tea snob and freelance edits for a living (MichelleLevigne@gmail.com for info/rates), but only enough to give her time to write. Her newest crime against the literary world is to be co-managing editor at Mt. Zion Ridge Press and launching the publishing co-op, Ye Olde Dragon Books. Be afraid ... be very afraid.

www.Mlevigne.com
www.MichelleLevigne.blogspot.com
www.YeOldeDragonBooks.com
www.MtZionRidgePress.com
@MichelleLevigne

Look for Michelle's Goodreads groups:
Guardians of Neighborlee
Voyages of the AFV Defender

NEWSLETTER:
Want to learn about upcoming books, book launch parties, inside information, and cover reveals?

Go to Michelle's website or blog to sign up.

Also by Michelle L. Levigne

Guardians of the Time Stream: 4-book Steampunk series
The Match Girls: Humorous inspirational romance series starting with **A Match (Not) Made in Heaven**
Sarai's Journey: A 2-book biblical fiction series
Tabor Heights: 20-book inspirational small town romance series.
Quarry Hall: 11-book women's fiction/suspense series
For Sale: Wedding Dress. Never Used: inspirational romance
Crooked Creek: Fun Fables About Critters and Kids: Children's short stories.
Do Yourself a Favor: Tips and Quips on the Writing Life. A book of writing advice.
Killing His Alter-Ego: contemporary romance/suspense, taking place in fandom.
The Commonwealth Universe: SF series, 25 books and growing
The Hunt: 5-book YA fantasy series
Faxinor: Fantasy series, 4 books and growing
Wildvine: Fantasy series, 14 books when all released
Neighborlee: Humorous fantasy series
Zygradon: 5-book Arthurian fantasy series
AFV Defender: SF adventure series
Young Defenders: Middle Grade SF series, spin-off of *AFV Defender*
Magic to Spare: Fantasy series

www.ingramcontent.com/pod-product-compliance
Lightning Source LLC
Chambersburg PA
CBHW022008120526
44592CB00034B/744